Computer

Computer

Paul Atkinson

REAKTION BOOKS

To Dad, for inspiring me to learn

Published by Reaktion Books Ltd
33 Great Sutton Street
London EC1V 0DX, UK

www.reaktionbooks.co.uk

First published 2010

Printed and bound in China by Eurasia

British Library Cataloguing in Publication Data

Atkinson, Paul.
    Computer. — (Objekt)
    1. Computers — History.
    2. Computers — Social aspects.
    3. Computer engineering — History.
    I. Title II. Series
    004'.09-dc22
    ISBN: 978 1 86189 664 3

Contents

Introduction: Computer Histories

To many people, computers are not the most interesting of objects. For most, they are devices to be used and enjoyed, not to be analysed and critiqued. The majority of users encounter computers either in the form of a desktop PC, a laptop, or as a multifunctional device combining a handheld computer with a media player and a mobile phone. They are familiar, quotidian products that are now taken for granted. But one only has to observe the ways in which people use computers, and the excessive extent to which they use them, to see just how valued they actually are. The electronic computer is such a massively useful and important tool that it has in many ways become an extension of ourselves. Computers enable us to carry out and organize our work, provide us with entertainment, store our memories and, increasingly, allow us to communicate with the rest of the world. To those who use them regularly, life without computers would be completely unthinkable. In fact, society has become so dependent upon the electronic computer, that future historians will no doubt regard it as the most significant technological product of all time.

But these historians will have problems.

Significant elements of the history of the computer are indistinct. For one thing, the rapid and continuous progression of computing technology means that any individual computer is, by its very nature,

ICL 2903, 1973. Over 3,000 of these popular 'small business' mainframe computers were sold.

a transient, ephemeral, fleeting object. Computers are, as one critic poetically put it, 'quickly orphaned husks of sand and plastic'.[1] And there are few products more completely obsolete than an obsolete computer. Discarded without a second thought, many models of computer have been tossed into the dustbin of history, and will never be recovered. The physical size of computers, coupled with the vast numbers of different designs produced, means that even if they were not discarded, a comprehensive physical collection of past products is completely unfeasible. And of course, to many people (including some historians), the physical design of the computer has been of little or no interest.

Many histories of the computer are concerned purely with charting the unrelenting progress of technology, painstakingly comparing the capabilities of improved machines to their predecessors. Clock Speeds and chipsets, Floating Points and FORTRAN. Written primarily for the knowledgeable specialist, such texts are impenetrable to the

ICT 1301, 1962. A decimal (rather than binary) computer that covered 700 square feet (65 square metres) and weighed over 5 tons.

majority. Other histories document the rapid global growth of the computing industry, providing economic and political analyses of the births and deaths of various corporations. Markets and mergers, targets and takeovers. But in describing the development of computing from such perspectives, these accounts pay no attention to the computer as an object. There are no detailed descriptions of their designed forms – the machines at the centre of their discourses barely even make an appearance. In fact, it is not uncommon for such histories not to contain a single image of a computer. It is almost as if an unwritten ruling has been agreed – that the material and visual aspects of computers are of no relevance whatsoever. At completely the other end of the scale are purely visual 'histories' of the computer: eye-candy collections of photographs displaying the changing form of the computer over time, but explaining little and questioning nothing.

Of course, all of these different histories are of value to their intended audiences. Taken together, they cover a huge subject area in great detail while individually proposing their own historical timelines of computer development. But the problem with these different timelines is that invariably they do not tally. The inconsistencies highlight the fact that there is, after all, no 'agreed' history. Computers purported to be of vital importance to the development of computing in some timelines are conspicuous by their absence in others. Some agree on the significance of certain breakthroughs, but attribute those same breakthroughs to different people or institutions. This is, in retrospect, completely understandable. The different approaches to the history of the computer are bound to elevate one aspect over another, and view achievements as being of different value. Any history will have its limitations, and in the history of computing, one of the most significant limitations is the simple fact that the very word 'computer' means different things to different people. Computer engineers might consider the word 'computer' as referring only to a microprocessor – the silicon chip inside an enormous range of everyday products from watches to washing machines, from mobile phones to microwave cookers. They would be completely correct in this, and yet the majority of non-specialist users relate the term 'computer' to a general-purpose information-processing machine in the form of a personal computer or PC. In fact, the problematic definition of the term lies at the root of a well-known difficulty in the history of computing: the title of 'the first computer'.

The seemingly simple question 'which was the first computer?' is in no way a straightforward one to answer. As one computer historian put it, 'there is no such thing as "first" in any activity associated with human invention. If you add enough adjectives to a description you can always claim your own favourite.'[2] This is most certainly the case with the electronic computer. Is the question what was the first mechanical computer? Or electro-mechanical? Electronic? Digital? Automatic? Large scale? General purpose? Programmable? Stored program? Commercially sold? Serially produced? All of these terms, and many others, have been used alongside the word 'computer' in order to make a specific claim to have developed the first one. And if the adjective of a particular claim is removed, the claim fails completely, leaving the way open for much older machines to be considered.

One might well ask why is it considered to be so important to determine who invented the computer. The answer is a mixture of national pride and ego. Being acknowledged as the country or person responsible for the creation of such a powerful and important invention invariably carries considerable kudos. Consequently countries have battled to stake their claims, and the bitterest rivalry has historically been between the US and the UK. There has been strong competition to claim the title of being 'the father of computing' on both sides of the Atlantic, with the earliest nomination being from

the UK. Charles Babbage's conception of mechanical computers pre-dated the electronic computer by more than a century, and his achievements are widely celebrated. US historians have argued that as it was a Hungarian-born American called John von Neumann who came up with the concept of a stored program computer (a machine that could retain both its own instructions and data), as well as the architecture on which today's computers are based, he (and therefore America) is the rightful 'father of modern computing'.[3] Others have argued that although he didn't use the same terminology, the British mathematician Alan Turing came up with the concept of a stored program computer over a decade earlier, with his theoretical vision of what is now referred to as a 'Turing Machine'.

IBM Ledger Card computer, 1974.

In terms of actual machines built, many current books still claim that the American ENIAC, completed at the University of Pennsylvania in 1946, was the first electronic computer; despite information coming to light in the 1970s that in fact the British Colossus, built at Bletchley Park in 1943, pre-dated it by more than two years. Other sources claim that the modern electronic computer did not appear until a stored program computer was finally built, which happened at Manchester University with their Manchester 'Baby' built in 1948. The competition develops further for the claim of the first serially produced commercial computer. Here, there is a real tension between developments in the US and the UK, along with a good deal of confusion over timing. Most sources agree on the year being 1951, but a great deal happened in computing that year. In the UK, Ferranti Ltd developed the Manchester 'Baby' into the Ferranti Mark 1, which was delivered in February. Remington Rand, having bought the Eckert-Mauchly Computer Corporation, which developed the UNIVAC, 'delivered' the first one in March 1951, although it wasn't 'dedicated' until June. There is confusion between computers discussed as 'commercial' (that is, sold to a customer) and serially produced, which puts an earlier electro-mechanical German computer by Konrad Zuse (a one-off made in 1944 and sold in 1950), and the American BINAC (a one-off built in 1949, sold to a customer but which never worked properly when installed) into the same frame. More confusion creeps in with the title 'the first business computer', which is often claimed for the LEO I, the Lyons Electronic Office developed from the Cambridge EDSAC machine of 1949. The LEO I was demonstrated to Queen Elizabeth II in February 1951, but was only used in-house from November 1951 until the LEO II was developed for sale in 1954.[4]

The dates quoted for the 'first' computer, then, are manipulated data that sometimes refer to different definitions of a machine, sometimes to the machine being completed and at other times being delivered (sometimes months before being made to work for the customer). In the case of the first UNIVAC, the first was signed over to the customer in 1951, but remained in the factory for demonstration purposes for so long that the second machine was built, delivered and installed in June 1952 before the first was actually shipped in December 1952. So what date should be used when determining a 'first'? Conception or realization? Order or sale? Completion in the factory? Delivery to a customer? Successful installation? There is no agreement on this issue, which makes a definitive timeline impossible. It has to be accepted, therefore, that for such complex technological products there is no relevant, single 'first' – rather, there is a series of related innovations, taking place in different locations, often at very similar times, each having a claim to having pushed the development of computing forward in one of a number of ways. A single, chronological, historical account of computing, then, would not only be problematic, it would also not be very useful.

While the concept of 'firsts' is not actually that useful when discussing the computer, it is still perhaps of interest to consider how historians have attempted to 'classify' them into different 'generations'. Many of these generational models have rather predictably been based around technological differences, yet others have been based around differences in the ways in which computers have been utilized or even the ways in which they have been commercialized. Historians of science and technology have conventionally classified computers into three, or sometimes four generations based on significant technological innovations.[5] At its most basic, a computer consists of a series of very fast switches, and the classifications usually run along the lines of a first generation of computers where those switches took the form of vacuum tubes (also referred to as 'valves' or 'thermionic valves'). Second-generation computers are usually defined as machines where the switching was carried out by transistors, with a third generation that employed integrated circuits and (if further divided) a fourth that contained microprocessors. These developments had a significant effect on the appearance of computers, particularly with respect to their physical size, yet this has not normally been an issue discussed in describing the history of the computer.

In the mid-1980s, a more accessible model of classification based on the use and perception of computers was proposed. Through the analysis of advertising material, changes in the representation of computers were assessed and it was surmised that there were significant distinctions in the way computers had been perceived over the course of their history. These distinctions led to a three-generation model of computing development. The first generation was defined as 'the computer as calculator', the second as 'the computer as an

Foxboro Fox 1 computer system, 1971. Computers were not always boring beige boxes.

information processor' and the third as 'the computer as a tool for revolution in the office'.[6] More recently, an alternative model identified four major turning points in the commercialization of computing technology. These followed the transformation of the computer from a scientific instrument to a commercial product in the late 1940s, the emergence of small systems in the late 1960s, the move to personal computing in the 1970s and finally to networking in the mid-1980s.[7] Both of these models are, of course, fuzzy at the generational boundaries, and also open to interpretation.

Modular Computer Systems Modcompclassic, 1978.

One problem with the historical approaches and generational models described above is that they tend to portray the history of the computer as a simplistic, sequential series of events. They suggest a very linear model of progression: one of continual miniaturization and incremental improvement; a logical chain of innovations; or an inevitable consequence of economic and political forces. In reality, the model of development has been far more fragmented, even erratic, with many alternative forms of computer being simultaneously created and marketed, only for many of them to be cast aside when the very users they were aimed at rejected them. The reactions to computers of those who use them have rarely been considered in constructing historical accounts, and yet they have proved to be of huge importance. It is clear from the evidence that the history of computing has been largely socially constructed rather than technologically determined.

Harris Corporation 6024 computer system, 1974.

That is the approach taken by this book. In contrast to technical or economic histories, it considers the electronic computer from the perspective of design history, and explores the computer as a designed object – a socially and culturally constructed artefact. As such, it investigates a number of different questions. Where did the initial form of the computer come from? Why did it appear the way it did? How did people first react to the computer? Why did computers take on so many different guises, and why did they then disappear? Did the design of computers affect the social relations of their users or vice versa? What stylistic influences came to bear on their design and why?

This book uncovers the physicality of computers, and reveals the surprising variety of their past forms. Computers went from being a daunting room full of cold, grey steel cabinets into an enormous

West Hyde Data-Screen Terminal, 1973. The computer as power tool: the cases of management computers were often dressed in wood effect finishes to distinguish them from those of lower-grade operators.

Hewlett Packard HP 250, 1979. Science fiction influences the office environment.

Orb multi-user business system, 1983.

range of different products, appearing in a multiplicity of wildly different and highly stylized physical forms. Before they became injection-moulded merchandise, sheet steel computer casings were painted in bright blues, reds, oranges and greens – colours which look strangely incongruous compared to the restrained and limited palettes of computers today. They were also used as power tools. Some manufacturers dressed the angular metal forms of computer terminals in mock wooden finishes in order to connote managerial status. Others built computer terminals into executive furniture, and yet other forms of computer indicated status by breaking away from the desk altogether and becoming portable. The introduction of plastics for computer casings in the late 1960s enabled more fluid forms to be realized, and freed designers to create more organic structures, reflecting the zeitgeist of the space race. At a point when their precise use was not yet fixed, these factors worked together to mark the computer out as an immensely exciting piece of technology that had the potential to shape the future. Yet from this position as an embodiment of opportunity and status, computers became standardized and sanitized everyday objects – truly global, mass-produced commodities. The story of that transformation is a fascinating one – a complex and forgotten history of vicissitude.

1 Polar Positions

The story of the development of the electronic computer from its initial form as a forbidding room-sized construction, and its transformation into an innocuous box sitting on top of an office desk, is a complex, convoluted one, which could, and indeed has, filled a number of books. But those two polar positions are perhaps the most interesting points at which to concentrate an account of the design history of the computer as a physical object. At one end of the scale is an awe-inspiring, esoteric piece of unfamiliar and potentially threatening new technology of huge magnitude, understood by few and feared by many. At the other end of the scale is a familiar, unobtrusive piece of everyday office equipment, understood by all and feared by none. A single operator sat alone at a control desk amid a large room of anonymous steel cabinets is a recurring image in early computing, contrasting powerfully with later images of users working alongside a smaller number of more human-scale units. The miniaturization of electronic components reduced the size of the computer beyond the imagination of early pioneers to a position where a stand-alone computer could be built into an office desk, and eventually placed within a single case which could sit on the desktop. The physicality of the computer has played a key role in defining the experience of operating the machine. We have moved

DEC Digital Datasystem, 1974. By the middle of the 1970s, terminals were presented as stand-alone word-processing computers able to fit comfortably on an office desk.

from working within the confines of the computer to working on computers wholly within the operator's grasp, and along the way our relationship to a fundamentally similar piece of technology has changed completely.

The vast majority of computers produced today are anonymous pieces of work. The result of research and development teamwork between engineers, programmers and designers, they are very rarely associated with particular individuals. This is, perhaps, not surprising given that the computer is now a quotidian commodity item, just one more product among the plethora of consumer goods we encounter every day. Earlier attempts to produce electronic computers, though, were much more bound up with the struggle to make significant breakthroughs; to realize theoretical aspirations; to shape the future of technological development. The pioneers attempting to do this were people driven – be it by personal ambition, intellectual

Ferranti Mercury, 1960. Operators of early computers often looked lost within huge rooms of equipment.

curiosity or national pride – into chasing a dream, of being the first to succeed where others had failed.

As a consequence of such fervour, early developments in computing are more often than not couched in the rhetoric of scientific discovery and heroic achievement. The enormous effort and resources required were channelled into a relatively small number of groundbreaking projects to create singular machines, and the narratives surrounding their creation are therefore closely associated with the particular individuals, teams and institutions pushing particular boundaries, and are understandably focused far more on the circumstances of their production rather than their consumption (which at that point was in any case limited).

Although it is the intention in this book to focus on the development of the modern electronic computer rather than to go back to the abacus and work forward (as many others have done) it would be inappropriate not to at least mention here the achievement and influence of Charles Babbage. In 1821 Babbage, a mathematician, and John Herschel, an astronomer, were consulting the manually calculated mathematical tables used at the time for all kinds of astronomical, engineering and navigational purposes, and found them to contain a significant number of inaccuracies. These errors were not only inconvenient, they were also fatal (one set of navigational tables was found to contain over 1,000 miscalculations and was believed to have caused many shipwrecks). Babbage concluded that if these tables could be generated by a reliable calculating machine, lives would be saved. Babbage was extremely well connected and highly respected in Victorian social circles, and he used this influence and a working demonstration model to secure large amounts of money from the government to develop such a calculating machine. His highly ambitious design for the 'Difference Engine', as he named it, called for an incredible 25,000 precision-engineered parts to be accurately assembled. After ten years of development work and constant reassurances that he was near completion, Babbage changed the design and started again. Infuriated, the government finally withdrew its support. The Difference Engine No. 2 was never completed in his lifetime and many critics believed that the design was beyond the limits of the manufacturing technology of the day. That notion was finally put to rest in 1991, when the Science Museum in London completed the construction of a machine to Babbage's plans using production tolerances achievable during his lifetime. It worked perfectly.

Babbage's reluctance to settle on a finalized design also meant that his plans for an even more ambitious, punched-card programmable machine[1] called the Analytical Engine were never realized, although it is now widely recognized that its design, consisting of stored memory and processing units, closely resembled that of a modern-day electronic computer. Consequently, Babbage is the earliest of the many contenders proposed for the title of 'the father of computing', setting a precedent in the history of computing for celebrating the conceptualization of a process as being of equal to or of more importance than its realization.[2]

Although they were largely the creation of a single individual, that Babbage's computers were products of the establishment is beyond question. As if it were created in direct response to the burgeoning industrial revolution, the Difference Engine was a physical manifestation of the division of labour,[3] and because of his approach to the processing of information and logical efficiency, Babbage 'embodied a link between calculating machinery and rational industrial management that has never since been broken'.[4]

Mechanical calculating machinery continued to be developed over the next century, resulting in a wide variety of machines that fall outside the scope of this book and are far too numerous to list

comprehensively here. The adoption of mechanical relays used in telephone systems led to important developments in analogue electro-mechanical computing, such as the German Konrad Zuse Z3 Computer of 1941 and electronic circuits were first used in the American, non-programmable Atanasoff-Berry Computer (ABC) of 1939. Both of these had an impact on later, programmable electronic computers, but that impact was not perhaps as significant as earlier work by Herman Hollerith. His doctoral thesis led to the design of the Hollerith Mech-anical Tabulator, which sorted data stored on punched cards. The machine was used by the US Census Office in 1890 and cut the time taken to collate all the census information from eight years to just one year. Hollerith's Tabulating Machine Company later became International Business Machines, better known as IBM – for many

Reconstruction of Difference Engine No. 2. The Science Museum's reconstruction of Babbage's Difference Engine proved that had it ever been built, it would have worked perfectly.

years the most important computer manufacturer in the world. IBM did more than any other institution in bringing the electronic computer to the world of business, but they did not invent it. As with so many other important inventions, the programmable electronic computer emerged from the pressures of war. Two different military requirements were highly influential in driving the development of computing forward during the Second World War. The first, with activity centred in the UK, was the need to decipher the enemy's coded messages for military intelligence purposes, and the second, with activity centred in the USA, was to speed up the calculation of ballistics information and produce firing tables with the same kind of accuracy Babbage had intended.

The Military Machine

What they did with Colossus, the first day they got it, was to put a problem onto it which they knew the answer. It took about half an hour to do the run. They let it run for about four hours, repeating the processes every half hour, and to their amazement, it gave the same answer every time. They were really amazed. It was that reliable, extremely reliable.[5]

The activities of code-breakers in the Second World War have been described in a number of factual accounts, but were widely popularized by Robert Harris in his 1995 novel *Enigma*, later made into a British movie. *Enigma* glamorized life around the grounds of the Buckinghamshire mansion that formed the base of secret cryptographic endeavour, and focused largely on the love interest between Tom Jericho, a brilliant young mathematician, and Hester Wallace, a worker at the base and a housemate of Jericho's former lover Claire, who has mysteriously disappeared. Their search for Claire uncovers a government plot to keep America in the war, and leads to the uncovering of a Polish spy they follow to Scotland, where the U-boat he is boarding is bombed.

A visit to the former site of the Government Code and Cypher School at Bletchley Park today, however, paints a less romantic picture. A tour around the decaying remains of the cold, cramped and damp huts in which the logging and decoding of intercepted messages took place gives one an appreciation of the dedication of the many hard-working staff in very difficult conditions, and makes their achievements appear all the more remarkable. Personal accounts of working there describe the bare concrete floors, light bulbs without shades, wooden trestle tables and broken electric stoves. 'It was dreadful . . . We all froze. We had to wear coats and mittens.'[6] Today, those bleak rooms form a fascinating museum displaying the equipment they used and describing their work in detail. The museum also has working examples of the many machines developed to make and break codes during the war, including a reconstruction of the first ever totally electronic computer. Because it formed part of such an important war operation, the story of its creation was for many years kept totally secret and it is something of a miracle that a reconstruction has been assembled at all.

Following the First World War, the Enigma cipher machine was developed by the German inventors Arthur Scherbius and Richard Ritter to overcome the limitations of previously used handwritten methods of encoding secret messages. The machine used an ingenious rotor system to scramble each letter of a message individually so that even if the same letter were keyed in twice in a row, the coded letters produced would be different. The sequence of the letters generated was dependent on the initial position of the rotors, and the three-rotor system in the Enigma machine had billions of possible initial positions, making the code extremely difficult (but not impossible) to break. Cryptographers at Bletchley Park used 'cribs'

– inspired guesses at the meanings of small sections of messages – to reduce the possible initial positions from billions to thousands, but these still required laborious checking to find the right answer. In 1940 the celebrated mathematician Alan Turing developed the work of Polish cryptographers to create an electro-mechanical code-breaking machine called a 'Bombe', which could check the thousands of possible variations and successfully decode Enigma messages within a few hours. There was, however, a higher-level code generated by a ten-rotor machine called the Lorenz cipher used for top-level strategic communications. Even with the use of 'cribs', the number of possible variations of initial settings within the Lorenz cipher was far too great for the mechanical relay-based Bombe machines to tackle. A mistake made by a German operator in sending a long message twice with the same initial settings enabled the logic of the code to be deduced, and armed with this information, Bletchley Park mathematician Max Newman (Turing's tutor at Cambridge) asked the Telecommunications Research Establishment at Malvern to produce an electronic machine to automate the method of finding initial code settings.

The resulting machine looked so eccentric in its construction that its operators named it 'Heath Robinson' after the famous illustrator of complex cartoon mechanisms. It was built at the Post Office Research Station at Dollis Hill, London, and used two paper tapes which ran on spiked wheels at speeds of 1,000 characters per second – one containing potential rotor settings and one containing the coded message. The Robinson machine worked well enough to prove the concept, but the paper tapes were not easily kept synchronized when running at the speeds necessary to decode a message within a reasonable time-frame. The spiked wheels kept ripping the paper. Another considerable problem was that the answer produced by the Robinson machine depended on an unreliable mechanical counter, and often, the answers given for the same message were different.

Because of these problems, Newman proposed an electronic computer to decipher Lorenz messages, but it was deemed unworkable. Because the Robinson machine was made almost completely from telephone switching components, Tommy Flowers, an electrical engineer at Dollis Hill who had impressed Turing during his work on developing the Bombe, was brought in to look at the problem. He said, 'I very soon came to the conclusion that it would never work . . . the paper wouldn't stand up to it'.[7] Flowers realized that the problem was similar to one he had addressed before the war in designing automatic telephone exchanges. What was required was at its most basic level an enormous collection of very fast switches. Flowers knew that electronic valves were capable of switching about a thousand times more quickly than mechanical relays. He had also made a major discovery about them:

> They wouldn't believe it. They were quite convinced that valves were very unreliable. This was based on their experience of radio equipment which was carted around, dumped around, switched on and off, and generally mishandled. But I'd introduced valves into telephone equipment in large numbers before the war and I knew that if you never moved them and never switched them off they would go on forever.[8]

Flowers's main contribution was to suggest that one of the synchronized paper tapes in the Heath Robinson machine could be replaced by a pattern generated electronically by valves, removing the synchronization problem and enabling reliable high-speed operation.

The officials at Bletchley Park were sceptical and would not back the development work. But Flowers was so convinced of its potential that he spent £1,000 of his own money and ten months designing and building the Colossus electronic code-breaking computer. It contained 1,500 thermionic valves – more than any other electronic device of the time – and was delivered to Bletchley Park at the end of 1943. In its first test it successfully decoded a real coded message so quickly that a total of ten improved machines were ordered.[9] The Mk II Colossi built in 1944 contained 2,400 valves each and were five times faster. Collectively they decoded millions of letters of German messages, and it is estimated that the Colossus significantly reduced the length of hostilities by up to three years.[10] Sadly, at the end of the war, Flowers was ordered to burn the machines' blueprints and the Colossi were destroyed, 'as was all hint that the world's first programmable electronic computer had ever existed'[11] – apart, that is, from two of the machines, which it is believed ended up at the Government Communications Headquarters (GCHQ) in Cheltenham. These are rumoured to have been used to decode Soviet messages in the Cold War, but they too were dismantled in the 1960s. For many years, their very existence was denied, and the Official Secrets Act silenced those who had worked on them. History was repeating itself – Babbage, without the aid of mechanical devices, managed in 1854 to break the Vigenère cipher, which had been considered unbreakable for 200 years. It is believed he was asked by his friend Admiral Beaufort to keep the discovery secret to give the British an advantage in the Prussian War. Similarly, unable to discuss his wartime achievements, Tommy Flowers returned to urgent work on reconstructing national telephone networks, but had no opportunity to convince his superiors of the benefits of computers or his ability to design and build the first stored program computer, and the significant advantage of a capable and experienced team went unrecognized.[12] It was not until the mid-1970s that information started to come to light and academic papers began to be written about the Colossus, including one by Tommy Flowers himself.

The Colossus was a programmable computer and could be reprogrammed through hard wiring and a switchboard. It contained all

the elements of a modern electronic computer apart from an internal program store. As it was not a general-purpose machine but was built to perform a single task, the use of an expensive memory was not required. But it did prove that high-speed digital computing could be achieved reliably with the use of valve circuits. In fact, because of its parallel processing design, it was so fast that over 50 years later, modern Pentium-based PCs still took twice as long to do the same decoding task.[13] The shroud of secrecy surrounding the Colossus, though, meant that for a long time it was omitted from the history of computing and the acknowledgements for designing the first electronic programmable computer went instead to the USA and the widely celebrated ENIAC of 1946.

The Aberdeen Proving Ground in Maryland is the home of the US Army's Ballistic Research Laboratory. During the Second World War,

The Colossus Machine, 1943. The top secret Colossus computer built at Bletchley Park only became known in the 1970s.

this laboratory was heavily involved in the production of firing tables – booklets that were supplied with guns, enabling them to be accurately aimed. Without precise calculations to compensate for factors such as wind speed and ammunition characteristics, big guns were not effective, and great effort was placed in the preparation and correction of firing tables.

John Mauchly, who was a physicist directly involved in the production of these leaflets, proposed the building of an electronic computer to speed up and improve the process of calculating trajectories. Mauchly conceived and designed the Electronic Numerical Integrator and Computer (ENIAC) with significant help from a graduate student, John Presper Eckert, who worked out the necessary electrical engineering required. Both men worked at the University of Pennsylvania, and the ENIAC was built at the university's Moore School of Electrical Engineering. Despite concerns over the feasibility of the project, funds were sourced and the project began in July 1943 and took just under three years and $500,000 to complete. The ENIAC contained almost 18,000 vacuum tubes and covered a floor area of around 65 square metres. The concerns over the feasibility of the ENIAC were based around the known lifespan and reliability of vacuum tubes, or valves. Unlike Tommy Flowers, who realized that it was the constant switching off of the devices which caused the problem, Eckert and Mauchly expected the tubes to break down, and so ran the ENIAC on lower operating voltages which cut the breakages down to only two or three times in a week.[14] However, with repair times, this meant that the computer was still only functioning for 50 per cent of the time. It was soon realized that most failures occurred when the tubes were heating up or cooling down, and so the machine was left on constantly. This reduced the down time further, but it still blew tubes on a regular basis; its longest continuous period in full operation was a mere five days. When it worked, however, it was a revelation. An academic paper written shortly after its launch marvelled at its capabilities:

> A skilled [human] computer with a desk machine can compute a 60-second trajectory in about twenty hours; a differential analyzer [a mechanical analogue calculator] can produce the same results in about fifteen minutes; the ENIAC can do it in thirty seconds, that is, it can compute the trajectory of a shell faster than the shell itself flies![15]

Data could be fed into the ENIAC using the IBM punched cards, which by this time had become an industry-standard for data storage. The results of calculations could also be punched out onto cards, but like the Colossus, the ENIAC had no memory, and rewiring the computer to perform different calculations took a good deal of time.

ENIAC, 1946.

Programs sometimes took days (and occasionally weeks) to set up and be made to work properly, and involved the manipulation of numerous cables and switches. Often described as a 'general purpose' computer, it was in fact limited in the types of calculations it could perform, having been designed specifically to solve a very particular problem. Even during its construction, the ENIAC's shortcomings and the potential for improvements became apparent to its creators. Its lack of memory, its complex architecture and unreliability led to the consideration of alternative designs, but the ENIAC project itself was so far advanced it was continued anyway. Despite these known shortcomings, the ENIAC was widely publicized, which in retrospect was one of its most significant contributions. Despite its military background, the design had already been widely discussed in academic circles, and the fact that it never managed to prove its military value as it was not completed until three months after the end of hostilities meant that the army was keen to promote it as having value beyond a military context. Consequently, the ENIAC was the subject of wide press coverage, with even the British Admiral Lord Mountbatten praising the 'Brain with 18,000 valves'[16] and its potential for peacetime operations in an article in *The Times*. The *Times* piece caused a chain of responses from interested and concerned readers. Across the world, the perception that America had produced the first electronic computer was instilled in the minds of the public.

Stored Programs

The idea of giving the computer a memory to store instructions for both carrying out calculations as well as for the data used in them was 'unquestionably the most decisive step in the development of the modern digital computer'[17] and its significance was not lost on the scientists and mathematicians of the day. The race was on to construct a stored program computer, but as ever, the attributions for this original concept are not as clear-cut as might be imagined.

Alan Turing's leading role in cryptography during the Second World War is by now well-known. His story was the subject of a successful 1986 West End and Broadway play, *Breaking the Code*, by Hugh Whitemore. The play, and its 1996 adaptation for BBC Television, featured Derek Jacobi as the unconventional Alan Turing – feted for his genius but vilified for his homosexuality and eventually driven to suicide. He also played a pivotal role in the conceptualization and design of the modern computer. Turing had previously written a paper titled 'On Computable Numbers with an Application to the Entscheidungsproblem' in 1936, in which he proved that a conceptual machine (now referred to as a 'Turing Machine') could perform any mathematical function as long as it could be represented in the form of an algorithm. Turing demonstrated that a 'universal' computing machine was a possibility – a machine that could be re-configured to perform the function of any other computing machine. This abstract notion of a universal computer being able to solve any conceivable mathematical problem relied on such a machine having, in effect, an infinite memory in which both mathematical data and instructions for their manipulation are held. Although the paper did not use the exact terminology, this is taken to be the first description of a stored program computer.

Another leading mathematician involved in the development of the stored program electronic computer was the Hungarian-born American John von Neumann, who was Professor of Mathematics at Princeton University. Turing and von Neumann met when Turing visited the Institute for Advanced Study at Princeton, and von Neumann invited Turing to work as his assistant for a year. As it happened, the war intervened and both men turned their talents to helping the war effort. Turing returned to Britain to work on code-breaking and von Neumann acted as a consultant to the Manhattan Project, constructing the atomic bomb. As a result of the enormous amount of calculations required for this project, von Neumann became highly interested in the potential of electronic computing. He started to attend meetings and lectures at the Moore School of Electrical Engineering, and joined in discussions about the ENIAC and its limitations. Aware of Turing's writings,[18] von Neumann could see the potential of a stored program computer, and after extensive discussions with four colleagues (including Eckert) over the course of a year, wrote a document laying out the design and architecture of such a machine – the Electronic Discrete Variable Automatic Computer (EDVAC). The 'First Draft of a Report on the EDVAC', written in the spring of 1945, proposed the use of binary numbers and the use of a mercury delay line[19] to store instructions and data, and became an incredibly important document in the development of computing. The computer architecture[20] laid out in this report forms the basic structure of almost every computer designed since. To ensure the report would not be restricted for security reasons, references to specific classified devices were deliberately omitted, and the descriptions of the EDVAC design it contained were theoretical and generic, which meant it was of limited use to the engineers trying to use it to build actual machines. In comparison, a report written by Turing later the same year referenced the 'First Draft' report, but gave such detailed descriptions of the circuits, specifications of the components required and how to achieve a working design (including the costs) that an extensive series of programs for the machine could be prepared and entered onto punched cards before it was even built.[21]

Turing was taking advantage of a new opportunity to resource the development of a stored program computer. At the same time that the American team at the Moore School of Electrical Engineering were working towards the EDVAC, the National Physical Laboratory (NPL) in Teddington started a Mathematics Division to explore the development of computing devices. The Director of this division, John Womersley, had visited the American projects, and used the 'First Draft' report to persuade Turing to join NPL in 1945 as a way of creating the machine he craved. Because of the Official Secrets Act, Womersley was unaware of the development of the Colossus, and of the fact that having seen the machine, Turing was just waiting for the right moment to develop those ideas further.

Turing's detailed design study for a stored program computer was outlined in his report 'Proposed Electronic Calculator'. Although the report referenced the American 'First Draft' report, Turing's design for a machine called the 'Automatic Computing Engine' (ACE), as a tribute to the work of Babbage over a century earlier, actually took a very different approach, and used a completely different computer architecture. Put very basically, the architecture of computers such as the EDVAC (and hence of the computers of today) aim to solve complex mathematical problems by using very complex machines which are relatively simple to program. In contrast, Turing's view was that it was better to solve problems through the application of careful thought than by using more complex machinery. The ACE design solved complex problems by using a very simple (and therefore much faster) machine which was relatively complex to program. Compared to the 18,000 valves in the ENIAC, the design for the ACE used only 2,000. Even the initial prototype version of the machine, the 'Pilot ACE', which used only 800 valves, was many times faster in operation than any other computer not only of its time, but for many years afterwards.[22]

Although the design of the ACE is now recognized as a revolutionary success, its realization was anything but straightforward, and a series of delays seriously jeopardized the whole project. Womersley commissioned the building of the ACE to the Post Office Research

Station at Dollis Hill, London, and Turing knew the previous work there on the Colossus by Tommy Flowers's team would be of huge value. At least their experience gained through the war period would not be wasted. Unfortunately, because of the huge backlog of urgent work required for the rebuilding of the national telephone system (which at that time came under the auspices of the Post Office), Flowers could only spare two engineers who had worked on the Colossus, and this caused severe delays in its construction. Added to these delays, both Turing and the management of NPL kept altering the design of the machine, making the engineers' jobs more difficult. Possible alternative construction sites were explored at the Department of Scientific and Industrial Research and at Cambridge Mathematical Laboratory, but these did not materialize.

The project received a boost when Harry Huskey joined NPL from the ENIAC project. As many people at NPL considered the ACE to be

The Pilot ACE, 1950. Alan Turing's Automatic Computing Engine approached the solving of problems in a completely different way to computers of today.

too ambitious, Huskey proposed the building of a smaller version called the 'Test Assembly' to prove the design, which could be built more quickly within NPL itself. Turing was set against the idea as it would delay the building of the full-scale machine, and although it had the support of the management, a series of internal political struggles over which division should run the project created further delays. Disillusioned, Turing departed to take a sabbatical at Cambridge in the autumn of 1947 and in May 1948 left the project altogether and took up the offer of working on a similar project under his old tutor, Max Newman, who was now based at Manchester University. The Test Assembly was eventually built in the form of the redesigned 'Pilot ACE', which ran its first program on 10 May 1950, and following further development work was used to provide a commercial computing service from 1952. A full-scale version (called the 'Big ACE') was finally built at NPL in 1958, but this was far too late for it to have the impact it should have had. By then, the revolutionary design was outdated, having valves instead of transistors, and an old-fashioned mercury delay line memory instead of the more advanced magnetic core memory.

At Manchester University, meanwhile, Max Newman had obtained a grant of £35,000 to build a digital computer in 1946. Under the tutelage of Newman, and later Alan Turing, Professor of Electrical Engineering Frederic Williams and his assistant Tom Kilburn together built a test-bed computer for a new type of memory, the 'Williams Tube'.[23] Although it was nowhere near as advanced a concept as the ACE, the Manchester Small-Scale Experimental Machine (also known as the 'Manchester "Baby"') ran a simple 17-line program on 21 June 1948 and in the process became the first stored program computer. The design was improved, with input from Turing, and with the addition of a number of components became the Manchester Mark 1, completed in October 1949.

Commercialization

The mind-blowing potential of previously unthinkable calculating power and the opportunity to prove complex, abstract theoretical problems beyond the capability of the human mind were reasons enough for scientists and mathematicians to conceive and develop these early electronic computing machines. However, such large-scale computers were significant projects, instigated at enormous cost by military institutions, government bodies or international corporations having extensive resources, or were the result of extensive research endeavours at universities funded by considerable research grants. These institutions were accountable to their paymasters, and consequently, the machines they funded were expected to justify their development costs by providing revenue-generating services. Computer time was at this point a rare and valuable commodity, and as such, the capabilities of computers were commercialized before computers were themselves. This practice had already been established in the development of the electronic computer's predecessor, the electro-mechanical calculator – large, complex assemblies of mechanical components based around the electro-mechanical relay, an electrically operated switch using a small

The Manchester Mark 1, 1949. The race to build the first stored program computer was won by Max Newman's team at Manchester University.

electromagnet to make or break a number of contacts. Apart from being far slower in operation than the switching carried out by vacuum tubes or 'valves', relays were noisy. One observer described the sound of an electro-mechanical calculator in use as sounding like 'a roomful of ladies knitting'.[24] A well-known example of such a machine was developed by Howard Aiken, a postgraduate physics student, who in 1939 proposed an 'Automatic Sequence Controlled Calculator' which attracted funding of hundreds of thousands of dollars from the President of IBM, Thomas Watson, along with the engineering resources of the company.

Completed in 1944 at Harvard University, the IBM ASCC, or Harvard Mk 1 as it was more commonly known, was 16 m long, 2.4 m high yet only 61 cm deep. It contained 500 miles (805 km) of wiring connecting 765,000 components including 3,500 relays. Its programs were stored on long loops of punched paper tape having 24 channels of information. Despite this complexity, it was incredibly reliable, and worked continuously day and night for over fifteen years, mainly providing ballistics calculations for the US Navy. The complexity of the Harvard Mk 1, though, was dwarfed by IBM's last great electro-mechanical machine, the Selective Sequence Electronic Calculator (SSEC). Only four years after the ASCC, this hybrid machine had 21,000 relays and 12,000 vacuum tubes, and ran for four years in IBM's main showroom in New York, where it could be watched by passers by, providing calculations for high-profile clients such as the US Atomic Energy Commission, calculating the position of planets and stars, including tables of the position of the moon which were later used to plot the course for the 1969 Apollo moon landings.[25]

The first generation of electronic computers started in the same position of providing a service; from the Colossus breaking wartime codes, through the ENIAC calculating firing tables, to the Pilot ACE providing a wide range of solutions on a commercial consultancy

basis for defence, ordnance survey and traffic simulations, and from calculating the earth's magnetic fields and aircraft stability simulations for the aircraft industry to producing PAYE tables for the Exchequer and train timetables for British Railways.[26] When IBM launched its Model 704 Electronic Data Processing Machine in 1957, a newspaper article reported:

> The machine will be hired out by IBM to anyone in Europe who wishes to make use of it – Government departments, international organizations, industries, and business firms. Also, a fund of £100,000 is being set aside by IBM to enable mathematicians and scientists engaged on pure research to make use of the machine – which is very costly to operate – free of charge.[27]

The IBM ASCC (Harvard Mk 1), 1944. An electro-mechanical forerunner of the electronic computer.

IBM SSEC, 1948. IBM's showpiece electro-mechanical machine was located in their showroom in New York and watched by passers-by.

Computer time was prohibitively expensive for many potential users, to the extent that one day's operation of the Pilot ACE easily covered the annual salary of the person who supervised its operation.[28] It is not surprising, then, that although the calculating power of the computer had proved itself to be of potentially great value in business applications, the dominant conception at this point was that a computer would never be anything other than a hugely expensive, centralized device, which would be built to order and maintained and controlled by specialists. Even the Director of the National Physical Laboratory himself, a Sir Charles Darwin, stated in 1946 that a single computer would probably be sufficient for the whole country's problem-solving requirements.[29]

The first step in changing this perception of the computer was to turn it into a commercially available machine to meet individual business user's needs, circumventing the need for companies having to pay for expensive consultancy services. Historians of computing have seen the early stages of the commercialization of the computer as having been driven initially by national-security customers and later by cost-sensitive commercial customers who were already well-established users of punched-card equipment.[30] US national security projects such as Air Defence and Atomic Energy Research provided the funding for the development of many of the technological advances that were exploited by later commercial machines, including magnetic tape and magnetic drum storage devices, ferrite-core memory and semiconductors; whereas the existing business market for traditional punched-card equipment had funded the development of closely related components of computer systems such as printers, card punches and card readers. However, even though these national security projects led to physical computing equipment, some of which were made and sold in multiples, these were not, strictly speaking, commercial machines made for open sale.

Although previously unavailable accounts now detail the top-secret development of the Colossus code-breaking computer prior to the ENIAC, computing historians are right to note that 'what is unique about the ideas generated by those associated with ENIAC is that they were freed of their military security classifications'.[31] The resulting publicity, along with the widely disseminated content of the 'First Draft of a Report on the EDVAC', greatly helped the University of Pennsylvania to initiate commercial demand for electronic computers. Unfortunately, adopting a new policy requiring all patents arising from sponsored research to be assigned to the University lost them the chance to become a significant player in commercial computing. Eckert and Mauchly, the mainstays of the ENIAC and EDVAC projects, left to found the Electronic Control Company (the first company founded expressly to produce electronic computers, later renamed the Eckert-Mauchly Computer Corporation) and instead developed the successful UNIversal Automatic Computer (UNIVAC) in 1951. Like the ENIAC, the UNIVAC received wide press coverage when it started to appear in the workplace, and 'it so caught the public's imagination that the words "UNIVAC" and "computer" became synonymous'.[32] As well as selling to government departments such as the US Census Bureau[33] and various military divisions, Eckert and Mauchly had long targeted insurance firms as potential customers for the data recording, processing and sorting capabilities of their computers, and when the Eckert-Mauchly Computer Corporation was taken over by Remington Rand and became their UNIVAC Division, sales to insurance firms were widely publicized. Images of parts of the UNIVAC being hoisted up the face of skyscrapers even appeared in daily newspapers.[34] For a machine containing over 5,000 valves, the UNIVAC was very reliable, with customer statistics showing it to be working 81 per cent of the time, helping to reassure potential customers of the value of investing in computing machinery. From a user's perspective, the revolutionary aspect of the UNIVAC was its use of tape-drive units to store data, which gave it the ability to automate many procedures that normally involved the physical moving of large numbers of punched cards by hand. This led to computers being referred to as 'tape machines' and even 'electronic brains', as they knew where to find information and what to do with it.[35] Between the first to leave the factory in 1952 and its replacement by the UNIVAC II in 1958, 46 of the original UNIVAC model were installed in businesses across America.

The potential market for commercial exploitation of computing technology was clear, and other research and government computers were also reconfigured into commercial concerns, some pre-dating the UNIVAC, but not sold on quite the same scale. The first of these was the 1949 Manchester Mark 1, which the British firm Ferranti developed with Manchester University staff Tom Kilburn and Frederic Williams, producing the commercial version sold as the Ferranti Mk 1

UNIVAC, 1951. Like the ENIAC it was developed from, the UNIVAC received wide publicity.

in February 1951. Seven of a slightly revised version (the Ferranti Mk 1* or Ferranti Star) were sold.

A physicist at Cambridge University, Maurice Wilkes, attended some of the same Moore School lectures attended by von Neumann in 1946, and based on these designed the Electronic Delay Storage Automatic Computer (EDSAC), which in 1949 became the first 'practical' stored program computer. From 1950, this machine provided a regular computing service to industry, and in 1951 it was taken up by a food company, J. Lyons & Co., and developed into the LEO Mark 1 (Lyons Electronic Office), becoming the first commercial computer designed specifically for business administration purposes. Applications of the LEO 1 Machine included important jobs such as calculating the required ingredients for and planning the following night's production and delivery schedules, including the associated invoicing. Later, in

The Ferranti Mk 1, 1951. Ferranti Ltd developed the Manchester Mark 1 into a commercial machine.

1956, it carried out the calculation of payrolls for external clients (as the UNIVAC had done a couple of years earlier), and led to Lyons using a LEO Mark 2 machine purely to provide a bureau service.

The Pilot ACE developed at the National Physical Laboratory was taken into production by The English Electric Company in 1955 and marketed as the DEUCE (Digital Electronic Universal Computing Engine). More than 30 units were sold to a mixture of universities, industry (where it was used for, among other things, aircraft design) and various government departments. Although it was not a direct continuation, the design and architecture of the Pilot ACE was also used by Harry Huskey as the basis for the Bendix G-15 computer he designed at the University of California at Berkeley in 1954.[36] Alan Turing's design principles allowed the computer to be small – the size of a large refrigerator[37] – and faster than many competitors. From 1956, Bendix produced 400 of the G-15 before being taken over by Control Data Corporation in 1963.

From these first steps, a complete industry took shape with quite remarkable speed. In 1955 *Fortune* magazine reported on some of the

LEO Mark 1, 1951. Hailed as the first computer developed for business applications, the LEO also calculated the ingredients required for the next day's production of goods.

leading computer and electronics manufacturers as having annual sales revenues from $169 million (Burroughs) to $2.96 billion (General Electric).[38]

Design Theory

It might seem strange that the aesthetic theories of an interwar German design school, the Bauhaus, should have had a significant influence on the physical appearance of electronic computers produced a quarter of a century later, but they did. When the architect and design consultant Eliot Noyes first encountered the company that was to become his most significant client, the archaic corporate environment suggested there was a great deal of work to be done to drag IBM into the twentieth century.

> When I first met IBM the large main company showroom in New York was a sepulchral place, with oak-panelled walls and columns, a deeply coffered painted ceiling, a complex pattern of many types of marble on the floor, oriental rugs on the marble and various models of back IBM accounting machines sitting uneasily on the oriental rugs. These accounting machines, I might add, often had cast iron cabriole legs in the manner, I believe, of Queen Anne furniture . . . It said IBM about 12 times on the facade . . . It also said, 'World Peace through World Trade' and many other slogans . . . Upstairs the typical offices had green walls . . . It was design schizophrenia of the worst sort.[39]

IBM were not alone in being a well-established company moving from producing old-fashioned business machinery into producing the latest in electronic computers, and understandably in such institutions, there was an amount of tradition and precedent to overcome. As well as having to compete with the existing aesthetics of a company's previous products, the electronic computer had no aesthetic precedent of its own. As a new invention whose function was not clearly defined, there was no obvious convention to follow. The designers and builders of early scientific and military computers had had no particular reason to concern themselves with the aesthetic appearance of the finished assemblies. Function was the prime directive, and the open-rack units allowing easy access to valves and wiring were vital at a point in time when 'programming' a computer to perform a particular function involved the hard rewiring of circuits which could take hours or even days to complete. Enclosing the computer in an attractive casing was not a high priority. In fact, some components such as thermionic valves needed a good circulation of air, and they were often oriented horizontally to facilitate cooling, which made enclosures undesirable.

Yet even before there was a desire to neatly package computers to make them marketable, or a need to provide logical control panels to enable the computers to be operated by non-specialists, advantage was taken of the nature of electronic componentry in being able to be controlled remotely. Different elements of mechanical systems usually dictated where certain controls appeared on a machine. Rotating shafts had to be physically connected to handles, knobs had to be connected directly to mechanical switches, and oil lubricators had to be placed over the runners they were lubricating. There was a strong, purposeful correlation between the mechanical arrangement of the components and the manual operation of the machine, and function had a significant determining effect on form. Electronic equipment, on the other hand, could be controlled from a distance through appropriate electrical connections. The control of components located at different and distant points on a large electronic machine could therefore be drawn together, easing the operation of complex devices.

While ease of operation and maintenance were key factors in the appearance of early computers, it is nevertheless entirely possible that their inherent aesthetics as large, rational arrays of clattering relays and electronic apparatus connected with kilometres of circuitous wiring were as familiar – and even reassuring – to the scientists and engineers well accustomed to laboratory-assembled test systems and prototypes as they were unfamiliar and bewildering to the casual observer. In the same way that the precision-turned shafts, cogs, rotors and handles of Babbage's Difference Engine perfectly reflected the machine-tool aesthetics of the burgeoning Industrial Revolution, the rack-built assemblies of glowing valves and switchgear reflected the birth of the age of electronics. Because of the manufacturing infrastructure of the industries supplying the parts, such constructions of electronic components would have perhaps been unlikely to take any other form than they actually did, but all the same, they would have had significant resonance and meaning to their creators, reflecting the specialized professional worlds in which they lived, while simultaneously retaining an air of esoteric mystery to the wider public.

It is clear that these very early machines were not designed products as such, but complex assemblages of a variety of components put together under the direction of leading scientists and engineers as experimental pieces. The control panels or 'consoles' of machines such as the Pilot ACE built at the National Physical Laboratory in 1950 were initially collections of existing instrumentation in their discrete sheet-steel cases, connected together rather than built as a bespoke panel, even though earlier machines such as the IBM SSEC had large, impressive purpose-built control desks – possibly because it was known from the outset that this machine would be used significantly as a showcase of IBM's consultant services to industry, and would be seen in publicity and promotional material.

For experimental machines, the complexities of controlling these machines through such specialized means were not really a great concern as those doing the controlling were the very scientists and engineers involved in their creation. The move of the computer from the laboratory to a commissioned installation, however, meant controlling the machine had to be undertaken by outside parties, and the need for centralized, logical and understandable controls became highly important. For machines produced in limited quantities, these consoles were often built upon existing steel office desks – a use of off-the-shelf parts that in the Standards Western Automatic Computer (SWAC) even extended to using standard shower doors as the glass fronts of processor unit cabinets![40]

The move to serial production prompted the input of specialist designers who could look independently at this new phenomenon of human/computer interaction (long before the term was coined) and propose ways in which the inherent complexity of computing might be made more accessible to non-specialist operators. These machines were still extremely expensive and represented a significant investment by the purchaser, and the cost of considerable amounts of design work was therefore easily justified. It was this design work which brought the influence of the Bauhaus to bear. Although it had been closed for over 20 years, the Bauhaus notions of rationalization and standardization became evident in the design of computers in the late 1950s and early 1960s – firstly through Adriano Olivetti, who had long been encouraged by the ideas of the Bauhaus to consider all design activities of a company as a holistic activity;[41] and secondly through Eliot Noyes, who studied architecture at Harvard under Bauhaus founder Walter Gropius and tutor Marcel Breuer before becoming a design consultant to IBM.[42]

Adriano Olivetti had worked with design consultants since the successful illustrator and designer Marcello Nizzoli worked on Olivetti

adding machines in the 1940s.[43] Nizzoli created designs for the company's first electronic calculators, as well as for the Lexikon typewriter, and helped to establish a reputation for the company as a manufacturer of well-designed products. Adriano Olivetti initiated his company's long-standing arrangement with the architect, designer and writer Ettore Sottsass in 1958. Sottsass had been acquainted with the design ideas of the Bauhaus through his rationalist architect father and had studied them intensively. His first project at Olivetti was Italy's first electronic computer, the Elea 9003, completed in 1959. Design historians have viewed this machine as unique in that it was the first time that electronics were given a new appearance through design, the first time that new technology and a new product language were brought together.[44] Sottsass noted that in using the company's previous calculating machines, users pressed a single button and

Standards Western Automatic Computer, 1950.

caused a direct reaction when the calculator provided the result. In contrast, with a large computer, there was a much more complex relationship between user and machine in which there were a whole series of steps between initiating a process and the result – steps which were 'invisible and rather incomprehensible to the user',[45] and which could not be easily communicated. In Sottsass's view 'a new form had to be found which, by its nature, had to be more symbolic and less descriptive'.[46] In a later interview, he recalled:

> I became close friends with the son of Adriano Olivetti, Roberto. Roberto was the president of the electronic department that was just starting in 1959. We used to go out and have dinner and discuss for hours and hours about what could be done to make products that were nice and human for the user. Around that time, computers were something very new and were as big as a whole room, so we wanted to design tools that didn't scare or bore the workers.[47]

Sottsass aimed to help workers overcome their fear and distrust of electronic technology by creating an emotional relationship between the user and the machine. Sottsass's role went far beyond the design of single products, as he aimed to develop a new and intrinsic 'language' of electronics, which would remain valid as technology developed and society became more familiar with computers.[48] Sottsass achieved this with the Elea by designing a series of standardized rectilinear elements, which could be arranged in different ways within a room as opposed to the faceless grey cabinets that lined the walls of other computer installations. The cables connecting these elements were routed through aerial cable ducts, allowing the system to easily be reconfigured and expanded. Considering the ergonomics of the design, he reduced the height of the units to allow operators to see each other and make the machine more human in scale, and tied the component parts together with a symbolic and daring use of colour.[49] Befitting his training, this was modernist architecture writ small.

IBM's President, Thomas Watson Jr, similarly took design seriously, and had a close working relationship with the established consultant Eliot Noyes. Inspired by the examples of Olivetti and Braun in their use of design, Noyes took it upon himself to promote the value of such an approach at every opportunity. He secretly arranged for brochures of Olivetti and Braun products to appear unannounced on Watson's desk on a regular basis in order to reinforce the message of good design. It clearly had the desired effect, as when asked how he thought these brochures compared to IBM's own, Watson stated:

Olivetti Elea 9003, 1959. The first computer associated with a 'name' designer: Ettore Sottsass.

The Olivetti material was filled with colour and excitement and fit together like a beautiful picture puzzle. Ours looked like directions on how to make bicarbonate of soda.[50]

Noyes became IBM's Consultant Director of Design and was given the green light to put in place a complete corporate design programme in 1956. He set about surrounding himself with an elite team of design consultants, including graphic designers Paul Rand, Marcel Breuer and George Nelson, and architects and designers Charles and Ray Eames. Noyes's penchant for consistently high design standards really became evident as he created a set of standard specifications covering the form, colour and physical structure of all the company's products.

In conjunction with this approach of design compatibility, IBM's computer products were the first to consider the thorny issue of technical compatibility. One of the most significant factors holding the computer industry back at this point was the inability of different computers to work with each other. Computers from competing manufacturers were perhaps understandably incompatible, but often, so too were computers from the same manufacturer. Initially, this tied customers to not only individual suppliers, but individual computers, as upgrading their computer system proved to be unacceptably expensive. There was a customer-led driving force, then, to achieve some kind of standardization of computing technology, resulting in what was at the time the most costly, privately-funded research and development programme ever undertaken. The dominance of IBM in the computing industry at this point is hard to overstate, as staggeringly 'more than 70% of all computers in the world had been manufactured by IBM'.[51] They had immense resources – annual revenues of $3.2 billion – and so could take the risk of investing $5 billion in replacing all of its product line with a new family of computers.[52] In 1964 they announced one of the most successful and influential computer designs of all, the IBM System/360, which over the next five years doubled IBM's already huge computer product revenues. System/360 was a complete mainframe system consisting of a range of six processing units sharing the same computer architecture and 44 peripherals with standard connection interfaces. All the units were interchangeable and would work with each other, allowing users to cost-effectively upgrade their computer systems as and when they required without having to rewrite all their software programs. This was a significant advantage over IBM's competitors, who sold only independent, inflexible, small or large machines. The advantage was in fact so great, that 'System/360 became a worldwide standard that reshaped the computer industry and underlay its growth for more than two decades'.[53] Slowly, IBM's competitors were forced to follow suit, and developed products designed to be compatible with System/360 equipment.

Like the Olivetti Elea, System/360 units were rectangular, modular and could be arranged in a variety of ways. The design of the control panel was also similarly thought through to make it as ergonomic, clear and understandable as possible. As a manifestation of Noyes's standard product specifications, it was an exemplar of conformity, strongly reflecting IBM's corporate identity. Noyes's input created a logic and rationale to IBM products that were a direct result of the idealist Bauhaus concepts he had encountered at Harvard.[54]

An Alternative View

An unassuming low-rise building hidden away on land leased from Stanford University in California has, since the early 1970s, been home to many of the most radical and forward-looking thinkers in computing ever known. Today, one is far more likely here to meet staff in casual clothing, and arriving on roller blades than in stuffy business

suits in executive cars, and the relaxed and tolerant atmosphere is as far removed from the bureaucratic office of Scott Adam's 'cubicle world' (where his comic creation 'Dilbert' the computer engineer toils) as it is possible to imagine. Although certainly laid back, it has been incredibly productive. In fact, this institution, Palo Alto Research Center, or PARC, has been responsible for such notable innovations as the Ethernet, laser printing and most importantly the Graphical User Interface or GUI. Founded by the Xerox Corporation, the people at PARC changed forever the face of computing.

It may seem superficial to explain away the progress of the computer as it appeared in the workplace between the late 1960s and the early 1980s as a period of incremental development – especially taken in light of the significant technological developments that occurred

IBM System/360, 1964. IBM's rationalization of integrated computer systems made System/360 the worldwide standard for computing for over twenty years.

over the period. The capabilities of the computer in terms of its sheer processing power continued to obey 'Moore's Law', roughly doubling every eighteen months. This, taken along with the corresponding miniaturization of electronic components, allowed the production of ever more powerful, capable and smaller machines to appear on a regular basis. Over this period, a bewildering variety of computers were produced in various forms and in markedly different colours, perhaps as a result of an increasing number of manufacturers joining the fray, all trying to establish a precedence for the physical form of a machine, the precise uses of which were clearly not fixed. Different forms of computers were produced for different users doing different tasks. The input terminals in particular were markedly dissimilar. Those for large-scale data entry by multiple typists bore little or no resemblance to machines used for 'serious' scientific calculations, or to machines aimed at manipulating information to allow managers to make strategic managerial decisions. The sheer number of different products makes a complete chronology and documentation of computers impossible, but the evidence that remains in the form of archival brochures from manufacturers (the objects themselves and the majority of the companies which created them having long since been consigned to the dustbin of history) allows at least some analysis showing that the diversity of different physical forms of the computer grew steadily until it peaked around the middle of the 1970s. At this point, mainframe computers were still present, mini computers were becoming more popular, and the earliest 'portable' machines for specialist applications were starting to appear.

However, the fact remains that despite these technological developments and the changing size and form of the computer over this period, the experience of operating the machine from the user's perspective was not all that different. From the user's point of view, the biggest change was the replacement of the typewriter with a keyboard and visual display, as the cost of monitors reduced to a point where they became a standard part of all computers. Yet in terms of use, even this was not so great a change. Computers were still text-based devices that required training to operate and program using a learned language and syntax. This all changed when in the late 1960s and early 1970s a group of people saw an alternative future for the computer, and envisaged a different relationship between the human and the machine – one where computers could be used by anybody, and improve life for all.

Perhaps the most significant change in the perception of the computer, and the change which allowed many more people to make use of the computer as a productive tool, was the creation of the Graphical User Interface (GUI) as an alternative way of interacting with the computer. Interestingly, this was largely the result of a serendipitous assembly of forward-thinking and highly talented people working collaboratively in a single location at a particular point in time. As a corporation, Xerox managed to put together one of the leading research centres in computing of the 1970s and is consequently often seen as one of the most forward-thinking of manufacturing companies, albeit with a less than enviable track record of realizing the potential of its many innovations.[55]

In the late 1960s Xerox was an incredibly cash-rich company. Their launch of the Xerox 914 copier in 1960 had led to over $1 billion in sales by 1968, and it was hailed by *Fortune* magazine as 'the most successful product ever marketed in America'. That product made Xerox one of the 100 largest corporations in the United States.[56] As a result, management had the advantage of extensive financial resources stemming from its monopoly of the photocopier market and a very successful product line, but it was facing a number of serious threats to its core business. Patents it held around photocopying technology were soon to expire, competitors were starting to enter the market and break their monopoly, and its management could see that one day, digital technology might replace the need for photocopiers altogether. The Chairman of Xerox, Peter McColough, had an ambitious aim to expand the business and its rule over the copier market 'into the domination of a greater universe – "the office of the future"'.[57] Having no in-house skills to address these threats and opportunities, Xerox entered the field in 1969 by purchasing an existing computer manufacturer, Scientific Data Systems (SDS). Jacob Goldman, Xerox's chief scientist, saw this as an opening and proposed that Xerox set up an independent, high-quality research facility to meet the needs of SDS, and to support the aim of creating the technology for the 'office of the future'. This facility became the famous Palo Alto Research Center, or Xerox PARC.

The person brought in to oversee the Computing Science Laboratory within PARC was Bob Taylor, a well-connected ex-NASA employee who had put together the embryonic Internet 'ARPANET' linking four American Universities while working for the government's Defense Advanced Research Projects Agency (ARPA). Taylor had been in charge of a budget of millions of dollars to fund new computing developments, and so had been 'the single most important force in US computer research'.[58] As a result of this position, 'he knew . . . every significant computer scientist in the United States'[59] and Xerox used him, along with higher than normal salaries, to attract the best possible talent to PARC.

At this point, most of those considering the future of computing were promoting the development of 'timesharing' as the way forward. Prior to the appearance of timesharing in 1961, the only way to access a centralized mainframe computer was on a serial basis, or one at a time. A connection was made between a user's terminal and the computer, and the connection remained live until the user finished working, which prevented another user from simultaneously accessing the machine. In this situation, prioritizing access to computers was a real problem. Timesharing was a way of breaking up the continuous connection to the computer into a series of parts, so that it could deal with a number of different connections at the same time, in parallel. When the computer finished executing one command from one user, it could switch to deal with a command from a different user, giving the impression to each user that they had a dedicated connection. At ARPA, Taylor had been working on this problem, as well as on making computers more interactive, so that there was less of a delay between sending the command to the computer and the computer providing the answer. The problems were connected in that the only way to make expensive, resource-heavy interactive systems cost-effective was to allow multiple users access to the system, yet allowing multiple users meant the responsiveness to any particular user would be slower.

Taylor had allocated a significant amount of his ARPA budget to continue funding the work of Douglas C. Engelbart, a former Second World War naval radar technician, who was energetically exploring interactivity in his work as a researcher at the Stanford Research Institute (SRI). Engelbart strongly believed that computers offered much more than merely the ability to solve complex mathematical equations. He saw computers as able to organize and manipulate information – an ability which provided an opportunity to 'augment human intellect', enabling mankind to achieve great things. At SRI, Engelbart established the 'Augmentation Research Center' and set about his mission to show exactly what a system of networked interactive computers could achieve. He first publicly demonstrated his system in December 1968, remotely connecting two distant sites in San Francisco and the Stanford Research Institute in Palo Alto. In an incredible presentation that has become legendary in technology circles, Engelbart showed the future of human/computer interaction, displaying 'a remote network, shared-screen collaboration, video conferencing, hypertext, [and] interactive text editing'.[60] Taylor, who had for a long time held the view that computers should communicate with their operators through visual displays rather than through punch cards and paper tape, knew that in order for PARC to succeed in developing 'the office of the future', he had to bring Engelbart's ideas on interactive computing into his Computing Science Laboratory. Engelbart would not move, but eventually Taylor managed to persuade Engelbart's close colleague, Bill English, to accept a post with the appealing remit of turning his theoretical work at SRI into a commercial product (something Engelbart's research centre had not achieved). English brought with him a dozen important researchers from Engelbart's laboratory, giving PARC all the experience and skills required to create an interactive computer of their own.

Douglas Engelbart is best known as the inventor of the computer mouse, the device so readily and unquestioningly accepted today as the only serious means with which to interact with a Graphical User Interface. What is perhaps less well-known is that the computer mouse was never originally intended to be used with a GUI at all, and in fact pre-dated the development of such interfaces by a decade. The mouse played a central role in the celebrated presentation of Engelbart's 'Augment System' in 1968, which has since become known as 'The Mother of all Demos'. A member of the audience of that demonstration recalled the effect of seeing the system in operation:

OMG! I was blown away. I couldn't quite bring myself to believe this was all for real. It was unbelievable. I'd never seen software engineering like it. We were working at the hammer and chisel phase of the Industrial Revolution, coding in assembly language, but here, these guys had invented machine tools à la Babbage. It was just mindboggling.[61]

The humble beginnings of the computer mouse stemmed from a series of specific experiments to explore the ergonomics of input devices. Receiving a grant from Taylor through NASA in 1963 to research 'light pens, tracking balls, and other kinds of gadgets',[62] Engelbart set up a series of experiments to test the time it took for operators to respond to on-screen stimuli using different devices. At this point, Engelbart remembered a complicated device he used as a student called a planimeter, and saw that a smaller, simpler device could achieve the same result by using two wheels fixed at right angles to each other. By rolling one of the wheels across the surface along one axis, the device could measure the distance the rolling wheel had moved in that direction. If the device was then moved along the other axis, the distance moved in that direction could be measured. If this dimensional information was then put into the computer, the movement and position of a cursor on a computer screen could be calculated. Bill English developed a prototype for

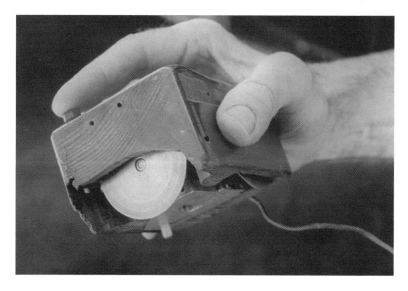

Engelbart and English's first mouse, circa 1963. The mouse was never intended to be used with a Graphical User Interface – that association came later.

Engelbart, which, when used in the selection experiments, 'just happened to win everything'[63] and became the favoured input device of all the subjects.[64] Engelbart applied a refined version of the mouse device to the Augment System in order to allow the on-screen editing of text. It used a three-button mouse, a standard 'qwerty' keyboard, and a chordset, which is an input device having five piano-like keys that can be pressed in different combinations to control different functions. Engelbart uses this arrangement to this day.

When Bill English joined Xerox in 1971, the project he managed aimed to reproduce Engelbart's Augment System on a large network of commercially available Nova 800 minicomputers.[65] The project was called 'POLOS', which stood for 'PARC On-Line Office System'. It was a large-scale prototype system, and was expensive. The main problem, though, was that Engelbart's interface system was difficult to learn. A series of dedicated command shortcuts using the chord-set had to be learned with the left hand, then the mouse positioned

The Augment System Interface, 1968. Years ahead of its time, Engelbart's 1968 demonstration of interactive computing took the computer industry by storm.

in the right place and a selection of text made with the right hand, then the edited text could be entered with the keyboard using both hands. Both hands constantly moved from sides to centre then back to the sides. For an experienced operator, the system was incredibly fast, but it took a long time (up to six months) to master.[66] English failed to make the arrangement of keyboard, mouse and chordset easier to use, but in conjunction with an external consultant, Jack Hawley, he did succeed in making a number of improvements to the mouse itself. Together, they developed a version that replaced the two wheels of his first mouse prototype with a single steel ball. This ball, when rolled in any direction, actuated two internal encoders at right angles to each other, and so allowed the measurement of movement in each plane simultaneously.

A competing project within Xerox called 'Alto' rejected the notion of a large, time-shared system, and instead focused on developing a small, interactive computer for individual use. As time went by, and the project gathered pace, it overtook POLOS completely. This project was influenced heavily by a maverick computer scientist called Alan Kay – a person whose radical, future-gazing views caused half of those who knew him to think that he was a crackpot and half to think he was a visionary.[67] This experimental high-end computer system, started in 1972, looked quite different to other computers used in offices. The main processing unit was small enough to fit underneath a table (causing one Xerox employee to nickname it the 'Gzunda' because it goes under the desk) and had a large, vertically oriented visual display based on an 8½" by 11" (22 × 28 cm) page. What made this machine stand out, though, was the display itself. The screen output was bitmapped – allowing black text to appear on a white background, just like ink on paper. What appeared on the screen was what would come out of the printer – an attribute which became known as WYSIWYG (what you see is what you get). With the text editing programmes written specially for it and the improved computer mouse from the POLOS project, this system formed the basis of Desktop Publishing. The cost of achieving this was seen as highly radical at the time, even within Xerox. The engineers from the now defunct POLOS project thought it was an incredible waste of resources to give everyone a dedicated 'personal' computer rather than multiple users accessing a single, large centralized machine, saying it would be like 'giving every secretary her own printing press when all she needed was a typewriter'.[68]

Only 2,000 Altos were eventually produced; some were used in various university departments, but many stayed within Xerox, where they were connected by an Ethernet network and enthusiastically used to communicate through electronic mail,[69] but it was never really successful as a commercial machine. The cost was too high, and its performance was too slow, especially when trying to cope with more difficult interfaces such as icon-driven systems developed by software engineer Larry Tesler, and trying to move overlapping 'windows' of documents on a 'desktop metaphor' display conceived by Kay. These first graphical interfaces worked so slowly that, when demonstrating them, Larry Tesler 'had to record it on videotape at one-ninth normal speed, so it would appear natural when played back in real time'.[70] Additionally, even by 1977 when the problems of speed and cost could be shown to have been much improved with the Alto III, the short-sighted managers of the manufacturing divisions of Xerox didn't want to add another item to their product line as it would prevent them meeting their year's sales targets.[71]

The failings of Xerox to bring the Alto and other inventions to market have entered computer folklore, with whole books dedicated to the episode.[72] As Steve Jobs once said, 'Xerox could have owned the entire computer industry today.'[73] Following a full demonstration of the system at PARC in 1979, Apple staff, including Jobs,

ICL helps shape the future

freely accessed much of the Alto technology. Many key Xerox staff then left PARC, among them Tesler, who took up an offer of working at Apple to replace their own attempts at a GUI with a version of the Alto interface. Xerox employee Brian Rosen left to set up Three Rivers Computer Corporation with former colleagues from Carnegie Mellon University and launched a commercial version of the Alto workstation called PERQ in 1980, which was distributed and later developed by the British company ICL.

Meanwhile, in 1981, Xerox finally launched a much-improved, easier to use version of a personal interactive computer called the 'Star' that the company had been developing since 1977. This had advanced software features which took Alan Kay's 'desktop metaphor' and developed it into a much more sophisticated 'office metaphor'[74] – a full Graphical User Interface with overlapping windows, and icons for files, documents and printers that was far in advance of anything else on the market. The processor cabinet was a similar size to that of the Alto, but the monitor display was a square screen of more familiar proportions. Despite all the advances, though, the Star computer was slow. Even one of its designers said it ran 'like molasses'. They were

Xerox Alto, 1972. The first computer to use a Graphical User Interface.

ICL PERQ, 1980.

also extremely expensive, with a retail price of $16,595, and only made economical sense as part of a system which 'required two to ten workstations, plus a high-speed laser printer and Ethernet to link it all together. That raised the per-user cost to at least $30,000, and the price of a whole, integrated system to a quarter of a million dollars or more'[75] – for anyone, that was a high-risk investment in untested technology. The market, it seems, was not ready for the Star. Sales reached a modest 30,000 units instead of the hundreds of thousands Xerox were hoping for. The Star's fate was finally sealed a few months after its launch when IBM released the IBM PC – a product that was as unimaginative, uninspiring and backward-looking as the Star was stunning and forward-looking, but at a fraction of the cost. IBM sold them by the millions.

Once at Apple, Tesler started working on the Lisa project, the development of which changed direction considerably after Apple staff's visit to PARC. Steve Jobs wanted a move away from earlier Apple designs to a single case containing the processing unit, monitor screen and disc drives with a separate keyboard.[76] This was implemented by industrial designer Bill Dresselhaus as a distinctive, horizontally

Xerox Star Computer, 1981. Too far ahead of its time, the Star was never the commercial success Xerox hoped it would be.

IBM PC, 1981. The unassuming IBM PC turned out to be one of the most important computers ever developed.

formatted unit, cantilevered forward over a smaller base, leaving room for the keyboard partly to fit underneath.

Prior to the design work on the Apple Lisa project, computer mice were inherently unreliable pieces of equipment, and because of their technical complexity, they were incredibly expensive to produce. The interior steel ball of the Hawley mice used on the Xerox Alto and Star was held in place in a precision-machined metal gimbal assembly that had to be precisely aligned with internal rollers and springs in order to work properly. This level of hand assembly meant a mouse could cost between $350 and $400 to produce, and as such, it was not suitable for mass production. Also, when in use the rolling ball collected dirt and debris from the work surface and transferred it to the internal rollers, which badly affected the performance of the mouse, and necessitated disassembly to enable it to be cleaned.

Consequently, for the Lisa mouse, Apple approached an established design team at Hovey-Kelly to solve these production and

Apple Lisa, 1983.

user-related problems.[77] The work they carried out, it has been suggested, was probably the most important in the history of the mouse (and consequently hugely significant to the wider acceptance and further development of the Graphical User Interface and computer itself):

> Apple's mouse actually was to its predecessors what the DC-3 was to the Wright Brothers' Flyer: not the first of its kind, but the breakthrough in technology and design that made possible a breakthrough in commercialization. Apple moved the mouse from the laboratory to the living room.[78]

The design team included Dean Hovey, Jim Sachs, Jim Yurchenco and Rickson Sun. Sun remembers Apple's Steve Jobs approaching them with a Xerox mouse, saying: 'Hey, what can you do to help me with this? I can't sell these for $350, but for $15 I could sell a ton of these.'[79] In typical fashion, Jobs was expecting a 90 per cent reduction in cost as well as a dramatic improvement in reliability.

Many of the engineering problems of reliability and assembly were solved by going right back to first principles. The steel ball within the Xerox mouse acted as a load-bearing part of the structure, which caused a number of problems. This was replaced with a 'floating' lead ball covered in rubber so that it didn't 'skid' across the paper surface, but rolled smoothly over it, held to the paper by its own weight. The assembly problems of having to precisely align a number of different parts were solved by developing a precision injection-moulded 'ribcage' which located and held all of the important internal mechanical components in the correct relationship to each other. These improvements turned the production of the mouse from an expensive, skilled-assembly job into a cheap, snap-together process.[80] Jim Yurchenco, who did the mechanical engineering of the Apple mouse, recalls:

The first ones they made were costing just under $20 to manufacture, so that was a major drop from the $350–$400 it originally cost to make. Now, of course, you can make a mechanical mouse for $2![81]

The design of Lisa's interface was also a major achievement. Apple's software designer Bill Atkinson had been developing an interface with static, full-screen windows and on-screen 'soft-keys', which could be clicked on using an optional mouse, but inspired by his observations of the Alto and Star graphical interfaces he and his team produced a fully mouse-based, icon-driven version with a drop-down menu bar, pop-up menus, trash can icon and 'drag and drop' overlapping

Apple Lisa Mouse, 1983. A stunning piece of design work turned the mouse from a hand-built, unreliable nightmare into a mass-produced, snap-together product that worked every time.

windows which expanded and contracted when double-clicked by the mouse.[82]

Although as a product, the Lisa was overpriced, slow and eventually unsuccessful, by the time it was launched in 1983 the Lisa contained a number of significant design advances that were utilized far more successfully a year later in the Apple Macintosh, which finally brought the computer mouse and Graphical User Interfaces to the mass market.

The story of the development and design of the Apple Macintosh computer has been told in great detail in numerous books,[83] which at least pay testament to its pivotal role in the history of the computer. Although there is a clear and expected bias in these texts, they are really not exaggerating when they point to the debt that the world of personal computing owes to the 'Mac'. Its potential impact was recognized early on in its creation, leading Steve Jobs to announce, in typically flamboyant style, that the Macintosh would 'put a dent in the universe'.[84]

The plastic casing of the Macintosh, designed by Jerry Manock and Terry Oyama, moved away from the Lisa's horizontal format, and placed the monitor on top of a floppy disc drive unit in a unique, single casing.[85] It was an idiosyncratic vertical form, quite distinct from other computers and 'as recognizable as a Volkswagen bug'.[86] This arrangement was largely to reduce the 'footprint' of the computer, making it take up less of the desk surface, but in the process it gave the Macintosh a strong product identity many reviewers have labelled as 'cute'. Much of the computer's appeal came from the aesthetics of the interface – the result of work by Apple graphic designer Susan Kare. Kare added details to Bill Atkinson's work which made the interface distinctive and refined, such as the pin-stripes across the top bar of windows, tinted scroll bars and designing idiosyncratic icons for the 'trash can' and 'bomb' which appeared if there

was a problem. She also designed the 'friendly Mac' icon – a smiling caricature of the computer that appeared as soon as it was turned on. As the front end of the first widely available GUI, Kare's work was hugely influential on their future development, and 'the happy-face Mac startup icon is still a universal symbol for the whole phenomenon'.[87]

Those in the computer industry responded well to its charms. The founder of Lotus Software, Mitch Kapor, said 'The IBM is a machine you can respect . . . The Macintosh is a machine you can love.'[88] Its toy-like appearance, though, coupled with its low performance, meant it was not taken seriously as a business machine.

Apple Macintosh Plus, 1986. Steve Jobs declared that the Macintosh would 'put a dent in the universe'.

It's a miracle that it sold *anything at all*. This was a computer with a single disk drive, no memory capacity, and almost no applications. People who bought it did so on seduction. It was not a rational buy. It was astonishing that Macintosh sold as many as it did.[89]

Because it was industry that provided an established market for sales, the Macintosh was quickly upgraded to have more memory (512k instead of 128k), but the slow sales of the first Mac and the huge investment already made in injection-moulding tooling meant that a redesigned and more successful version called the Macintosh SE with an internal disc drive and a 'refined' design by Frog Design's Hartmut Esslinger did not appear until 1987.

The Macintosh's idiosyncratic appearance is widely recognized and indeed has become an 'iconic' piece of design work. It did indeed put 'a dent in the universe', but that dent is in the shape of the GUI and mouse, not in the shape of the Mac itself. Third party developers quickly produced graphical interfaces for IBM PC compatible

A team at IBM testing the 'Topview' interface, 1985.

machines to make them act more like a Macintosh. By 1985 a number of alternatives were available. IBM produced their own version called 'TopView' which had pop-up menus, and Digital Research released 'GEM', which was so close to the Macintosh interface in appearance that Apple sued them. Quarterdeck Office Systems launched a version called 'DESQview', which allowed numerous programs to run simultaneously in different windows, just months before Microsoft produced the first version of 'Windows' in November 1985. The subversive and anarchic approach of the Apple Macintosh was subsumed into the

Compaq 'Deskpro 2000' PC, 1997. Despite the massive influence of the Macintosh, the design precedent of the IBM PC proved too difficult to overcome.

mainstream. By 1990, 'Windows 3.0' had reached a level of sophistication close to that of the Macintosh interface, and the commercial driving force of compatibility with an established installed base of PC machines meant that the size, appearance and more conservative format of the computer initiated with the IBM PC was set in place for many years to come. 'As the saying goes: "No one ever got fired for buying IBM".'[90]

2 Personal Matters

Do It Yourself

> Consider a future device for individual use, which is a sort of mechanized private file and library. It needs a name, and to coin one at random, 'memex' will do. A memex is a device in which an individual stores all his books, records, and communications, and which is mechanized so that it may be consulted with exceeding speed and flexibility. It is an enlarged intimate supplement to his memory.[1]

This visionary image is an extract from a widely reproduced article titled 'As We May Think' by the physicist Vannevar Bush. In it, he extrapolates the ways in which various technologies might develop to be of benefit to man, including instant image recording, speech recognition and relational data connections (now known as hyperlinks). It presents what at the time was a radical view of the potential benefits to the *individual*, rather than business, that could be afforded by computing technology. Surprisingly, it was written in 1945 – right at the dawn of the electronic computing era. As a driving force for progress, Bush's article was revolutionary, and inspired many to spend their whole careers developing computers to enhance human achievement rather than to just perform calculations. Yet for many years the aims of such people were met with disdain. Douglas Engelbart said that every time he told colleagues that individuals would one day own their own, interactive computers it was like 'proposing that everyone would soon have his own private helicopter'.[2]

There were a few people who shared views such as Engelbart's dotted around the industry, struggling to be heard, but the established computer manufacturers had no interest in developing computers for individuals. There were, however, many others who were not part of the establishment who were interested in exactly that. Without them, and the clubs they formed, the computer might well have stayed in the office. These people tinkered away at home in garages and sheds building computers that were 'marginal, esoteric, hobbyist' items.[3] They were the same enthusiasts who worked to assemble two-way radios and various other electronics projects, bent on mastering, adapting and subverting technology to suit their own ends. Because of this do-it-yourself, self-reliant approach, these machines had a particular aesthetic. Flat-panel surface-mounted toggle switches, buttons and lights; folded sheet-steel enclosures or handmade wooden boxes; screen-printed graphics and a tolerance of exposed parts and wiring: all marked the early home computer as the continuation of existing practices of garage/tool shed construction or at best, very low-volume production.

This involvement with technology for technology's sake is at the heart of one sociologist's view of the first home computers as 'self-referential' machines.[4] Even though manufacturers argued that without offering some real benefits 'people will not buy technology for its own sake',[5] home microcomputers became far more successful than they were ever expected to be – in spite of the first machines being able to actually do very little. So little in fact that the computing guru Alan Kay once wryly stated that 'hobbyists actually enjoyed their machines more when they were broken, because then they could actually do something with them'.[6] They had no software applications to run, and few peripherals with which to interact. Consequently, involvement with the home microcomputer was carried out purely to engage with computing technology itself. The home computer was, in fact, a machine for learning about computers.

Early home computers bore no resemblance to personal computers as they are known today. They were little more than collections of switches and lights connected to circuit boards, and the limitations of technology meant they performed only the most basic of calculating functions. Although not primarily intended to be a home computer or hobbyist item, the Kenbak-1 is considered by many to be the first personal computer (although the term was not in common use then). It cost $750 in 1971 – a year before the microprocessor chip was invented. Its designer, John Blankenbaker, gained his experience of computers professionally, having previously worked on the SEAC (National Bureau of Standards Eastern Automatic Computer) in early 1951 as a student at Oregon State College, and then as a graduate on the development of digital computers for the Hughes Aircraft Company. Blankenbaker found himself unemployed in Los Angeles in 1970 and became interested in creating a computer for personal use. In order to keep the cost down, the only input was through

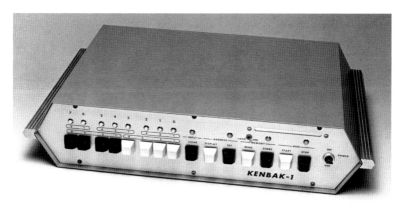

The Kenbak-1, 1971. Sheet metal casings and push button switches marked home computers out as hobbyist products.

panel-mounted switches on the front of the folded sheet-steel unit, and the only output was via a row of small lights. It had only 256 bytes of memory. Intended from the start to be an educational tool, it was marketed out of Blankenbaker's garage primarily to schools, but the lengthy budget cycles of educational institutions caused serious cash flow problems.[7] After selling only around 40 machines to a mixture of schools and interested individuals, the company closed in 1973. Even so, Blankenbaker successfully proved that a simple computer could be feasibly produced for personal rather than business use and could be privately rather than corporately owned.

Further evidencing the link between amateur radio and home computing, the Mark-8 Microcomputer was based on the world's first 8-bit processor, the Intel 8008, and appeared as a 'minicomputer' kit project (as the term 'microcomputer' hadn't been coined at this point) in the July 1974 issue of *Radio-Electronics*. The kit was the work of an electronics hobbyist, Jonathan Titus, who bought three of the processor chips and developed a panel with switches and indicators as a way of programming them. Once programmed, the device could then utilize a keyboard or monitor. Titus wrote an article on his project and sent it to *Popular Electronics*, who rejected it as they had a similar project almost ready for press. Beating them to it, their rival *Radio-Electronics* quickly printed the project as a cover story and caused *Popular Electronics* to put their own project on hold. The magazine advertised the kit and instruction book, priced at $55. The booklet explained that the machine's main function was for data manipulation, but that it could also be used for the complex programming of electronic calculators, teaching people how to program a computer, running an automated dark-room system, controlling laboratory experiments and collecting data, and even controlling and scheduling a model railway system.[8] The project generated huge interest in the readership, and thousands of the

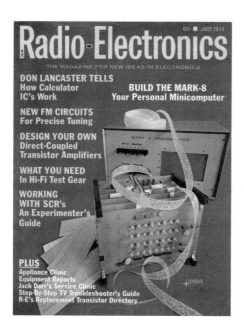

instruction booklets were ordered. However, the actual kit contained only the circuit board and plans, leaving customers to source all the components themselves (including the then expensive and hard to come by processor chips). As a result, it was not as successful a machine as it might have been, although it did show that to amateur electronics enthusiasts, the fascinating possibility of building and owning a computer of their own was rapidly gathering pace.

The mail-order computer kit that really allowed people to do it themselves, and the one that proved the existence of a potentially huge market for home computers, was the Altair 8800. Developed by Ed Roberts during 1974, it appeared on the cover of the January 1975 edition of *Popular Electronics*. This exposure gave a huge boost to electronics hobbyists desperately keen to learn about computers. Roberts had started out as an electronics hobbyist himself,

Radio-Electronics, July 1974.

but by the mid-1970s was an experienced businessman and part of an established network of companies involved in the sourcing and distribution of electronic components. The company he founded, Micro Instrumentation and Telemetry Systems (MITS), had done good business selling calculator kits for hobbyists, but afford-able calculators had become easily available, and the company now had financial difficulties. Roberts thought a mail-order computer kit might generate some money to ease the company's cash flow prob-lems. He based his computer design around the follow-up to the Intel chip used in the Mark-8, the Intel 8080. He anticipated selling 800 Altair kits in total and thought he might sell 200 in the first year, at which point the company would break even. At the same time, the editor of *Popular Electronics* was looking for a project to upstage the successful article on the Mark-8 in *Radio-Electronics*, and heard

Popular Electronics, January 1975.

about the Altair project. The magazine contacted Roberts, asking him if he could have the project ready by the end of the year, additionally requesting that it appear in an attractive cabinet so that it would be suitable as a cover story. Roberts strove to complete the project to the magazine's deadline to gain the benefit of the publicity. Through his network of contacts and his experience of negotiating low prices for the bulk buying of components, the full Altair kit cost only $397 including the sheet-steel cabinet, or $498 fully assembled. Within weeks MITS were inundated with orders. Selling an unexpected 200 units a day, the company was swamped, and struggled to meet demand.[9] It seemed that for the right product at the right price, the sky was the limit.

The runaway success experienced by MITS led directly to the first 'clone' computer. Advertised in kit form in the same magazine, *Popular Electronics*, in October 1975, the IMSAI 8080 was developed as a direct response to the unprecedented demand for the Altair, and was deliberately fully compatible with it. Like the Altair, it could run a 4K or 8K BASIC operating system, and could be easily used with peripherals such as floppy disk drives, printers or monitors. Users wrote their own software programs, such as simple data sorting, logic procedures and even a very basic chess game (in which each piece was presented on a monitor as just a code letter!). Around 20,000 units were sold, and reproductions of the original are still manufactured to this day.

Interest in these computer kits ran high among hobbyists, and the original Altair had been a major topic of discussion at the first meeting of the Homebrew Computer Club in March 1975, held in a private garage on the West Coast of California. The club's members had been impressed with the computer's design, yet could see a number of ways in which it could be improved and so started to develop their own alternatives. One member, Stephen Wozniak, who had been a ham radio operator and had been building electronic projects since

The Microcomputer System that's easy to take

elementary school, saw the cost of the microprocessor as a major obstacle. He developed his own computer that could do far more than the Altair, using the MOS Technology 6502 microprocessor chip. This was a readily available copy of the more expensive Motorola 6800 microprocessor and was by far the cheapest on the market. It cost less than one-sixth of the price of rival chips such as the Intel 8080 used in the Altair. Wozniak's design was an inspired piece of work. Rather than have switches and lights as inputs and outputs as on other home computers, Wozniak's computer used a keyboard to enter instructions and display the output on a monitor screen. He designed the machine over a six-month period, and with his friend Steve Jobs put together his first prototype by March 1976. They took the design firstly to Hewlett-Packard (HP), where Wozniak worked designing calculators. In one of the most staggering missed

IMSAI 8080, 1975.

opportunities imaginable, HP were not interested in manufacturing the machine, as they could see no future in making personal computers.[10] They gave free rein to Jobs and Wozniak to sell the computer, even though technically, as Wozniak was an employee, they actually owned the rights to the design!

Instead, Paul Terrell, the owner of a local computer store and part of another established business network, offered to sell the machines in wooden cases if Jobs and Wozniak could provide pre-assembled boards. The two entrepreneurs easily raised the capital to make enough boards for Terrell as well as an extra amount to sell directly themselves. They registered the company name 'Apple' on 1 April 1976, and launched the computer as the 'Apple I'. Many people wanted the computer, and sales soon soared. But in typical do-it-yourself fashion,

Apple I Computer, 1976. Owners built wooden cases themselves to house their Apple I computers.

rather than buy the completed assembly, the majority bought just the pre-assembled boards for $666.66 and made a case themselves.

Members of computer clubs were well used to taking this approach with electronics projects, frequently housing their latest creations in painted wooden cigar boxes. Proud owners made cases for the Apple I with varying degrees of skill and success, which was all part of the experience. It was the activities of such hobbyists that 'created a form of the micro which reflected their own values and was the machine they wanted to "consume".[11]

Although the market for these machines was clearly there, Apple's next product moved the home computer from being a self-assembly kit to an off-the-shelf item. Using the experience of designing the Apple I, feedback from members of the Homebrew Computer Club and money from selling around 150 of the boards, Wozniak designed a second, much improved computer using the same processor chip. Wringing more functionality from the chip than even the manufacturers thought possible, the Apple II (or Apple][as it was badged by Apple) had colour, high-resolution graphics, sound and the ability to add game controllers.[12] In fact, many of the features of the Apple II, especially its colour capability, came from Wozniak's love of computer games and after having designed the game *Breakout* for Atari (a job he landed through Steve Jobs when he worked there), he also wanted to be able to play it on a BASIC computer. The computer was designed in such an open way that anyone could view the code used to create any program to run on it. This led to a large number of do-it-yourself programs, mostly games, being written and distributed for the Apple II by a growing network of games enthusiasts, and many of these later formed significant software houses including Broderbund and Electronic Arts. The Apple II's ease of use and wide availability of software also led to the computer being widely adopted in schools and to the development of further educational software.[13]

Stephen Wozniak was happy to concentrate on the circuitry inside the computer. Steve Jobs, on the other hand, had his eye set firmly on the market. He always intended the Apple II to be a more professional-looking machine than the do-it-yourself, wooden-cased projects emanating from computer clubs. At the same time, he did not want it to be a cold, impersonal steel box like many of the business machines of the day. Jobs saw the Apple II as not being aimed at hobbyists who would mess with the internal workings, but at consumers who would view it as more of an appliance, and a significant amount of effort went into designing and producing a suitable plastic casing. This approach was timely, as other companies were also starting to take advantage of the interest in home computers and were attempting to appeal to general consumers rather than specialist hobbyists.

Including the Apple II, three products of this year were significant in the development of home computing, and are referred to as the 'Holy Trinity' of home computers. The Commodore PET (Personal Electronic Transactor), which used the same processor as the Apple I and II, came fully assembled and was the first all-in-one, self-contained home computer. It was easy to operate and had a built-in

Apple II, 1977. The spreadsheet software 'VisiCalc' turned the Apple II from a home machine into a vital business tool.

cassette drive, monitor and membrane keyboard. Tandy's entry into the computer market, the TRS-80, had the advantage of being sold directly from the company's well-established RadioShack chain of electronics component stores. This was a popular beginner's computer, as the manual assumed the user had no prior knowledge of computing. Ten thousand were ordered in the first month, where the company had projected sales of 3,500 units a year (one for each RadioShack store in the US). The most successful of this trinity, the Apple II, made great play of its colour graphics capability and was an instant hit with home users, most of whom connected the computer to their television sets instead of buying a monitor. As the majority of users had no experience of programming, they tended to buy software programs developed by third-party companies, and the majority of these were games programs. More useful applications that

Commodore PET 2001, 1977.

became available included programs for filing information, drawing simple charts and diagrams, and planning tax returns. By far the most popular piece of software though was Apple Writer. Published by Apple themselves, this was a simple word-processing program allowing home users to create professional-looking letters and reports. Famously, the 1979 spreadsheet software program 'VisiCalc' written by Dan Bricklin and Bob Frankston also made the Apple II an indispensable business tool. Financial managers, who would previously spend weeks producing complicated accounting forecasts, could suddenly see the effect of changing elements of a financial model simply by pressing a button. 'Thousands of business people bought Apple IIs solely because it was the only computer that ran VisiCalc.'[14] The Apple II, then, marks the point of convergence between home

Tandy TRS-80, 1977.

computers and office computers as discrete products. VisiCalc was incredibly influential in that it brought the trajectories of home computers and business machines together; eventually resulting in a universal machine that would fit both uses and could move between both environments.

The response by the big players in the computing industry to the Apple II was fast, and impacted on the whole computer industry. Until this point, IBM had seen only a specialist niche role for stand-alone, small computers, aimed squarely at the scientific market. Realizing the potential loss of sales across a wide range of business customers adopting VisiCalc and the Apple II, IBM were forced into producing a personal desktop computer so quickly that they used easily available, off-the-shelf components. The resulting IBM PC of 1981 had such an open architecture that other manufacturers easily copied it, launching a whole industry of IBM-compatible computers and leading eventually to IBM relinquishing control over much of the computer market. In fact, the only real winner was the company IBM commissioned to write the disk operating system that the IBM PC and consequently all its clones used – Microsoft.

The impact of hobbyist computer clubs on the mainstream computing industry, then, cannot be overstated. They attracted members whose day jobs were in large established electronics companies as well as those using computers purely as a leisure activity, and acted as a breeding ground for new ideas about computers that moved easily between the two environments. Members of the Homebrew Computer Club alone, which at its peak consisted of around 500 people, launched no fewer than 23 companies that eventually 'transformed the entire American economy'.[15] Key to the home computer's development, though, was the social environment in which it was created. Wozniak himself has discussed at length the excitement of seeing new prototype projects in the flesh, exploring them at first hand, asking involved questions of their creators and enthusiastically discussing possibilities with like-minded people in an informal setting. As he wrote once in an article about the Homebrew Computer Club:

> The Apple I and II were designed strictly on a hobby, for fun, basis, not to be a product for a company. . . . Schematics of the Apple I were passed around freely, and I'd even go over to people's houses and help them build their own.[16]

Without the counter-cultural mentality and social interaction of individuals in groups such as the Homebrew Computer Club, the Apple I and II would never have been created, and the history of personal computing would have been very different.

A Computer in a Briefcase

> Electronics in an attaché case will transform the hallmark of executive life. Designed by Honeywell, the case would allow a government scientist to carry with him a computer, a telephone with computer memory, a TV camera and monitor, and a TV receiver linked to a micro-storage file so a book page or other reference could be displayed at will. There is also a small space for medicines, contact lenses, playing cards. Feasible within three to five years; commercially available in ten to fifteen.[17]

By the mid-1960s, computers were still huge, unwieldy objects that more often than not took up whole rooms. The thought of being able to carry a computer around in a briefcase was outlandish. Ridiculous, even. But that is exactly what those working at the forefront of computing could see was eventually going to happen. The quote above is from an article in *Esquire* magazine in May 1966, reporting on the work of Stanley Kubrick in researching for his latest film project,

2001: A Space Odyssey. During this research he commissioned a number of major international corporations to predict what certain technological products would look like 35 years in the future. A concept design produced by the American computer manufacturer Honeywell showed their vision of how things would be. Their impressive suggestion was that a complete, self-contained computing system would become so portable that it would fit in a briefcase.

Computing technology, just as predicted in 1965 by Gordon Moore, has continued to increase in power and reduce in size at a set rate, which gradually made portable computers more of an actual possibility. As it turned out, the timing of Honeywell's prediction was remarkably prescient, but the roots of the portable computer as a real product (as opposed to inspired guesswork) arose from the 'Dynabook' interactive computer concepts produced by Alan Kay. Kay had conceptualized a computer aimed at children that brought together his work on interactive computing, the emerging technologies of flat-screen displays and handwriting recognition, and research into

Honeywell's portable computer concept, 1966. At the instigation of Stanley Kubrick, Honeywell were asked what computers would look like in the year 2001. Their answer was a computer in a briefcase.

simple programming languages he had carried out while studying for his doctorate at Utah in 1968. He had been developing a desktop personal computer since early 1967, and in the summer of 1968 gave a presentation of this machine and its unique software at the first ARPA grad students' conference. At this conference, Kay visited Donald Bitzer's lab where the first plasma panel flat-screen display was being invented.

> We saw a one-inch-square display that could light up a few pixels. Flat-screen displays were not a new idea either in fiction, semi-fiction (like *Popular Science* magazine), or in the real technological world. Still, it was galvanizing to actually see the start of one![18]

From his experience of developing a desktop computer, Kay knew the amount of transistors needed to create a portable computer, and using 'Moore's Law' estimated that it would be ten years before they could fit on the back of a suitably sized plasma panel. Later the same year, after visiting other groups of researchers working on computers that could be operated and programmed by children and on computers that would recognize handwriting, Kay came up with the concept of a portable computer that could combine all of these developments. When he arrived back at Utah, he made a cardboard model to see what such a machine would be like. He made it hollow so that it could be loaded with lead pellets to see how heavy it could be before becoming unacceptably weighty, and put slots on the side to represent removable memory components and to house the stylus that would be used to write and draw on the screen. It was certainly one of the most radical product proposals of the time, and Kay took the concept with him when he joined the Xerox Palo Alto Research Center (PARC) in 1970. Here Kay developed the concept further through Xerox's 'Learning Research Group', and the concept was

widely disseminated through conference papers and articles as 'A Dynamic Medium for Creative Thought':

> Imagine having your own self-contained knowledge manipulator in a portable package the size and shape of an ordinary notebook. Suppose it had enough power to outrace your senses of sight and hearing, enough capacity to store for later retrieval thousands of page-equivalents of reference materials, poems, letters, recipes, records, drawings, animations, musical scores, waveforms, dynamic simulations, and anything else you would like to remember and change. We envision a device as small and portable as possible which could both take in and give out information in quantities approaching that of human sensory systems.[19]

Kay's vision of the Dynabook was an incredibly powerful one. Although such a computer was not technically possible at the time,

Alan Kay's original 'Dynabook' concept model, 1968. One of the most influential computer concepts of all time.

it was convincing enough to inspire a number of people in the industry to work towards achieving a truly portable computer.

The Weight Issue

Alan Kay's dream of portable computers was that they should be devices that everyone, even children, would use. Manufacturers, on the other hand, knew that initially portable computers would be very expensive to produce, and so only really suitable for wealthy customers. There was a perceived need for business users to have instant access to information at all times, and this led to the first portable computers being aimed at travelling executives.

The earliest attempts at producing a computer in a briefcase appeared in the early 1970s, but these were only really portable computer terminals. They had no computing processing power of their own, but they could be connected to remote computers through a telephone by using an acoustic coupler. Portable terminals were used mainly by travelling sales executives to transmit sales figures and orders back to the office. However attractive a proposition they might have seemed, they didn't really deliver on the expectations of a portable computer. They were heavy items to carry around, and because of the size and high cost of monitors at this point, they lacked any kind of display technology. The only thing they could do was to use a small built-in thermal printer to produce paper copies of information. Two of the many players in this field were the American company Texas Instruments with their 'Silent 700' range, and the British company Transdata with their 'Portable Data Transmission Terminals' of 1972 and 1973 respectively.

The development of cheaper, reliable memory devices during the late 1970s facilitated a small improvement in portable computing. Machines such as the Texas Instruments '765 Portable Memory

Texas Instruments
model 725 portable data terminal

Terminal' of 1977 included 20K of a new solid-state technology called 'bubble memory'. This allowed for around four pages of stored data to be edited before it had to be transmitted over the telephone. However, although technically advanced, this was not really that significant an amount from the user's point of view, and there was still no display provided, which somewhat limited their usefulness.

The first really viable 'portable' computers were in reality 'as portable as a suitcase full of bricks'.[20] Appearing in the early 1980s, they were referred to as 'luggable' or 'transportable' rather than portable, and showed just how strong the desire for portable computers must have been to even contemplate carrying them around. The physical form these computers took was derived from another of Alan Kay's designs – the Xerox Notetaker. Kay and other members

Texas Instruments Portable Data Terminal, 1972.

Transdata Portable Data Transmission Terminal, 1973.

of his Learning Research Group were frustrated at the directions being taken by other departments within Xerox, and realized that the research and development required to bring the Dynabook concept to fruition was just not going to happen in the near future. In 1976 Kay, along with Adele Goldberg, Larry Tesler (a member of the Homebrew Computer Club) and later Doug Fairbairn, decided to go down a different route and develop a product that was somewhere between the futuristic concept of the Dynabook and the advanced but existing Alto computer created at Xerox some three years earlier.

Kay sketched out a design for a computer that could fit into a suitcase or on a user's lap, yet work in much the same way as the Alto in having a Graphical User Interface. Like the Dynabook, the project was considered by Xerox as looking too far ahead and so was not

Texas Instruments 765 Portable Memory Terminal, 1977.

supported, leaving the team to develop it themselves. As with the Dynabook, Kay and Goldberg maintained their vision of a computer that could be operated by children, and imagined the Notetaker being used as an electronic notebook, being taken to school for study and carried back to do homework. By the time a working trial product appeared, the computer had a very high specification, having a prototype 7" (18 cm) touch-sensitive display screen as well as a mouse, a microphone, stereo speakers, a rechargeable battery, a special version of the 'Smalltalk' graphical interface used in the Alto, 128k of memory and an Ethernet board to give it the ability to be networked. Unfortunately, when all this was squeezed into a single case, Kay was disappointed to find that the finished computer weighed over 20 kg. This meant there was no way it could be lifted by a child – it couldn't even easily be lifted by an adult! The Notetaker looked like a small suitcase when carried, with the screen and disk drives on the top, protected by a latched lid. However, the weight of the computer was such that it caused the case to warp when lifted by the handle. In use, it was laid on its side, with the screen and disk drives facing the user, and the lid, which was connected to the computer by a

Xerox 'Notetaker' prototype portable, 1978. Another influential concept from Alan Kay, the Notetaker was also ahead of its time.

flexible cable, folded down to form the keyboard. It was functional, though, and portable to an extent, and was successfully tested in use on board an aeroplane.[21]

In total, ten prototype Notetaker computers were produced, which proved that a powerful, portable device was a possibility. Xerox however, in a move that would become all too familiar, refused to put the Notetaker into production, and left others to take up the challenge. Of the pale imitations of the Notetaker that inevitably followed, the 'Osborne 1' computer is recognized as the 'the first commercially successful portable computer',[22] although like the Notetaker, its portability was highly questionable. Even the company's founder, Adam Osborne, himself estimated 'that at least 80% of his portables never left the office'.[23]

The creators of the Osborne 1, Adam Osborne and Lee Felsenstein (both also members of the Homebrew Computer Club), were well aware of the Notetaker prototype, and saw a gap in the market for a more straightforward computer that was small and sturdy enough for travel, easy to manufacture and cheap. Their first machine shipped in June 1981, but it was not much lighter than the Notetaker. A review article in *Design* magazine described the Osborne 1 as 'a brute . . . a 13 kg machine in a box the size of a small suitcase'. In essence, and quite unlike the Notetaker, the Osborne 1 was a more or less standard desktop computer with a proprietary text-based interface, placed inside a deep vertical case. It ran off mains electricity (an extra battery pack was optional), had 64k of memory, built-in disk drives on the top, and a tiny, 5 inch (13 cm) CRT display screen, which was difficult to see. Despite these limitations, the ready market for a portable computer of any kind meant that the Osborne 1 sold well. It helped that it cost a comparatively reasonable $1,795 and that it came bundled with a large amount of free software (which set a precedent for its competitors which exists to this day). At one point selling over 10,000 units

a month (when they expected to sell 10,000 over the product's lifetime) the Osborne Computer Corporation was one of the fastest-growing computer companies ever. But this accolade was a double-edged sword. As others before them had done, they struggled to meet demand and filed for bankruptcy in 1983. Their initial success, however, caused a number of competitors – ranging from start-up companies such as Kaypro and Compaq through to more established companies such as Commodore, and even the 'Big Blue' itself, IBM – to quickly produce visually very similar products, mostly having a larger 9" (23 cm) screen and more memory, but weighing more or less the same. Over the next five years, the sheer number of manufacturers creating products imitating the Osborne 1 suggests that as far as they were concerned, the future shape of portable computing had already been decided. The customers who had to try to carry them about, though, had different

Osborne 1, 1981. Despite being massively heavy, the success of the Osborne 1 caused competitors to copy its design.

views and it was not long before their weight and size made all these units fail as a product type. Attention turned instead to a much more acceptable form of portable computer – the laptop.

Laptop Computers

The laptop computer we are so familiar with today was the result of a seemingly unreasonable request. A highly-placed executive who had received one of the few sophisticated Xerox Alto computers to have been sold was talking to John Ellenby, a British computer scientist at Xerox PARC who had worked on its design.

He told me the Alto was great, but that he had stopped depending on it as he couldn't take it with him to where problems needed solving. I said I could make one the size of a suitcase – he said 'no – make it half the

IBM Portable Personal Computer 5155, 1984.

size of my briefcase'. That's where the aim for the size of the GRiD computer came from. He gave me the belief that there was indeed demand for a powerful, really portable computer.[24]

Although it was considerably more expensive than any other portable computer of the time, the 'Compass' computer that resulted from this request was streets ahead of the competition in every respect. It was a machine that finally delivered everything that a travelling executive required of a portable computer, technically and visually.

Ellenby believed so strongly in the potential of such a device that he left Xerox and set up his own computer development company, GRiD Systems. He invited Bill Moggridge, a leading British design consultant who had recently arrived in California, to set up an American branch of his successful London-based office, to work as part of his product development team on the industrial design and mechanical engineering of the computer.

Throughout 1979, Ellenby and Moggridge held long discussions about what a small, portable computer might look like and the various technologies that were converging to make such a machine possible. Based on these discussions, Moggridge produced a conceptual model to be used to persuade venture capitalists to finance the project. This neat and compact unit had a rubberized keyboard and a small numerical keypad next to an off-centre display, which was intended for telephone dialling. To protect these, the product folded in half across the centre (which is now referred to as a 'clamshell' design). The form began to alter when detailed product development started and the selected technological developments were taken into account.

The most important of these technologies was the display. The design team chose an impressive prototype electro-luminescent display by Sharp, which could cope with graphics as well as text. Next came

the low-profile keyboard, which manufacturers suddenly reduced in depth by half to only ¾ inch (2 cm), allowing a slim casing to become a realistic possibility. The very latest developments in computer chip design were exploited, as was the use of a newly developed storage technology called 'bubble memory'. A decision was made to provide 256K of memory, which sounds a small amount now, but was considerably more than any other portable computer of the time. This amount was considered to be more than adequate because the intention was to use a then radical system called 'GRiD Central' and have information resident on a centralized server. The user would dial

GRiD Concept model, 1979. A concept for a computer that folded in half to fit inside a briefcase inspired the first laptop as we know them today.

Initial sketch of the GRiD 'Compass' Computer, 1980.

in to the server using the built-in modem and upload or download any files they wanted to store or retrieve.

Another significant factor in achieving the look and feel of the finished design was the choice of magnesium as the casing material. The case needed to be light, robust and be able to conduct large amounts of heat away from the power supply. Even though magnesium was expensive, the weight of the final product was considered to be far more of an issue to the target market than its cost. Strangely, the extraordinary strength needed for the product arose not from its intended use, but from the choice of maintenance strategy planned for the 'Compass' computer. GRiD intended to guarantee a 24-hour turnaround repair service, which meant the computer would have to be transported by a parcel courier. To test the forces the computer would have to survive, an accelerometer was packaged up and sent across the world by courier. When the package finally returned, the readouts showed that it had been subjected to impact forces equivalent

GRiD 'Compass' Computer Model 1101, 1982. Labelled 'the Porsche of computers', the iconic form of the GRiD 'Compass' has informed the design of laptops ever since.

to being dropped 1.2 m onto a concrete floor! In order to create a suitably rugged product that could withstand such a force, the design team had to work with a chainsaw manufacturer to develop the precise, thin-wall castings required.

Although the design of the 'Compass' was rugged, its appearance was deliberately meant to be very prestigious and elegant in order to appeal to a high-level executive customer. Worldwide, this was potentially a large market that had a requirement for sophisticated, portable information processing and that would also be able to afford the high price. The 'Compass' retailed at $8,000, which was more than double the cost of an equivalent desktop machine. Unfortunately, this proved to be a price that the majority of customers could not justify. It became a niche product, selling to a small number of executives from the 'Fortune 500' companies, but not in anywhere near enough quantities to repay the venture capitalists. There was an urgent need to find an alternative market, and fortunately, the computer's rugged design specification turned out to appeal to a very different audience. The American Forces bought a large number of specially adapted computers for use in the field; NASA bought them for use on the space shuttle; and they were fitted into 'Airforce One' aeroplanes for the President of the USA. This exposure gave the 'Compass' an iconic status as an exclusive product. The Museum of Modern Art in New York placed it in their permanent design collection; *Business Week* magazine dubbed it 'the "Porsche" of computers'; and the Industrial Designers Society of America gave the GRiD 'Compass' computer the award for Design Excellence in 1982 for 'substantially advancing the state of the art of computer design'.[25]

While it was John Ellenby who saw the ways in which bringing together a number of different cutting-edge technological developments could actually create the ideal portable computer, the concept of a small, powerful portable computer had been accurately imagined a decade earlier by Alan Kay. Consequently, it is probably fair to say that had the GRiD 'Compass' laptop computer not been developed during 1980–81 the laptop would have arrived sooner or later, although not necessarily in the same form. It would be difficult, though, to overstate the influence of the design of the GRiD 'Compass' computer. At the time, it was radically different as a product, and it set a precedent for the visual identity of the laptop that has remained ever since. It was copied so widely that licences and royalties from the intellectual property contained in the design of the patented hinge and 'clamshell' casing generated far more revenue than sales of the computer itself ever did. In solving the problem of how to protect the keyboard and screen when not in use by adopting the 'clamshell' form, the designers also created an iconic sign in which the shape and the ritual of opening the product reflected that of an actual briefcase. Over a quarter of a century later, the vast majority of laptop computers on the market have the same form, are roughly the same size, and have a similar aesthetic appearance as the original 'Compass'.

The longevity of the physical form of the laptop masks a significant amount of diversity. As with any other form of computer, the internal technology has become steadily smaller and more powerful, yet the external arrangement of components has remained almost static. Some new technologies have been included – most notably 'trackpoint' buttons, trackballs and more recently, trackpads, which have been developed to replace the need for a mouse. Stereo speakers and built-in webcams have also appeared on some models, yet the differences between various laptops remain fairly superficial, with the styling and the specification of processor and memory being the key differential between a wide range of target markets. It seems that every class of user is infatuated with the laptop, from top-level executives through to schoolchildren. They are used for every situation, from business meetings to playing movies for entertainment. At the time of writing, the Information Technology business website *ZDNet* lists reviews of 5,181 different models of laptop computer, separated into twelve different categories including budget models, business laptops, desktop replacements, netbooks, rugged laptops and ultra-portables.

In fact, the form of the laptop has proved to be so acceptable in answering the needs of different users that it is not surprising that it has formed the basis of attempts to try and disseminate computing to some of the world's most inaccessible places. Motivated by a wildly different objective to that which drove the development of early 'executive' portables, the One Laptop per Child (OLPC) programme is an altruistic move to provide computing facilities for children in the developing world. It emerged from the Massachusetts Institute of Technology's Media Lab under the direction of Nicholas Negroponte. Amongst others, the project involves Seymour Papert who was involved in developing 'Logo', the first programming language specifically designed for children, which in turn inspired Alan Kay in developing his influential 'Dynabook' concept in the late 1960s. Negroponte and Papert have been involved in bringing computing technology to children in remote rural areas since the early 1980s, and in January 2005 Negroponte developed the concept of a $100 laptop to distribute to the poor children of the world.[26] Initially supported by the microprocessor manufacturer AMD and Google and quickly followed by other supporters, the concept was presented at the World Economic Forum (WEF) in Switzerland and received extensive worldwide press coverage. The original idea was to reduce costs by employing a cheap rear-projection screen rather than an LCD display, and use free open source software for the operating system. The concept included WiFi and 3G connectivity, achieved through 'mesh networking' where the laptops connect to each other to form a reliable network. The intention was to provide between 100 and 200 million laptops by the end of 2006.[27] A mock-up model of folding black panels was intending to employ 'parasitic power' generated by tapping the keys, but this was soon replaced by the so-called 'Green Machine', a rugged 'clamshell' design with a built-in cranking handle to generate power.

Reliability issues around the crank handle forced a redesign, and Yves Behar of fuseproject created the XO laptop for OLPC, which appeared in 2006. The XO-1 production version featured a built-in carrying handle, solid-state flash memory so that no moving parts are required, and a sealed rubber membrane keyboard to keep out dust and water. The battery-powered unit could be charged using external solar power or manually powered units.

The plan to persuade governments to purchase over one million units each was only partially successful, as costs rose beyond those initially projected and attention was in places diverted to providing more basic facilities seen as more urgent.[28] A well-received alternative plan

XO-1 Laptop from 'One Laptop per Child', 2006. A low-cost laptop for the world.

called 'Give One, Get One' in North America and Canada encouraged individuals to buy two of the machines for $399 on the proviso that one of them was donated to developing countries. Negroponte then pinned his hopes on the successful reception of the XO-2, a dual-screen product more like an electronic book.[29]

The OLPC project, along with other recent developments aimed at slimming down the laptop to a more basic form to reduce the cost – such as the educationally aimed Asus Eee PC (with its tagline 'Easy to Learn, Easy to Work, Easy to Play') – signalled the move of the laptop to finally cover the whole spectrum of possible users, including the children that Kay's 'Dynabook' concept always intended to support.

Tablet Computers

The ability to write instructions directly onto a computer screen had long been the aim of many computer engineers, and provided a separate line of development that created a product in many ways even closer to Kay's original vision of the 'Dynabook' than the laptop computer. Tablet computers (or tablet PCs) are characterized by large, touch-sensitive screens operated using a stylus or finger and by having the ability to recognize a user's handwriting. Operating a tablet PC by writing onto the screen is a process referred to as 'pen computing'. When tablets first arrived on the market towards the end of the 1980s, they caused enormous excitement in the computer industry, and venture capitalists flocked to invest money in their development. *Business Week* magazine predicted that sales of such machines could hit $3 billion by the year 2000.[30] The industry was convinced that pen computing was going to be the next big thing, and by the start of the 1990s, every major computer manufacturer (as well as a number of promising start-up ventures) had some type of pen-based machine under development.

The innovation of the tablet computer brought together three completely separate and unconnected areas of research into a single device: the development of pen interfaces to interactively operate computers, the development of handwriting recognition hardware and software, and the development of touch-sensitive screens.

Although users today don't give a second thought to using a mouse with a keyboard to operate a computer, the pen was actually one of the earliest alternative input devices to be developed once computers had gained display monitors. Light-sensitive pens could detect the light emitting from a Cathode Ray Tube (CRT) and be used to point to items directly on the screen. This principle was employed in the experimental 'Whirlwind' computer at Massachusetts Institute of Technology (MIT), which was built to analyse aircraft stability for the US Navy between 1946 and 1949. A symbol representing an aircraft was displayed on the monitor screen, and when the light pen (or light gun) was pointed at it, the computer would display identifying text about that aircraft. This machine contained around 5,000 valves, was the first computer to operate in real time and to use video displays as an output. It went online in April 1951 and formed the starting point for the later, transistor-based TX-0 machine started in 1953, and the far larger valve-based SAGE (Semi-Automatic Ground Environment) Air Defence System started in 1958; both developed at MIT's Lincoln Laboratories.

The SAGE system consisted of a series of computers that, containing 53,000 valves and covering over ½ acre (2,000m²) each, were the largest computers ever built. Each of the operating consoles contained a large, circular Cathode Ray Tube (CRT) display, at which the operator would observe 'blips' showing the location of an aircraft or missile. If a light gun was pointed at that point on the screen, an internal photocell registered the blip. Since the time taken for the screen display to be refreshed was a known quantity, the time difference between the start of the screen refresh and the light gun registering a blip could be translated into an accurate X-Y position, and a trajectory could be predicted. As a serious piece of equipment on which the security of the nation might depend, it says a great deal about the social practices of the time that the console also contained a built-in cigarette lighter and ashtray!

The TX-0 machine was the first in a series of experimental digital computers built at MIT, which included the 1958 TX-2. Though it was never intended for this purpose, a doctoral student called Ivan Sutherland used this machine in 1963 to develop 'Sketchpad' – the first ever computer-aided drawing software. Sketchpad allowed the 'direct manipulation' of computer data, and Sutherland's revolutionary PhD thesis became highly influential in the fields of computer graphics and human/computer interaction:

SAGE computer system, 1961. Covering over 1/2 acre each, SAGE Air Defence computer systems were the largest ever built.

The Sketchpad system uses drawing as a novel communication medium for a computer . . . A Sketchpad user sketches directly on a computer display with a light pen. The light pen is used both to position parts of the drawing on the display and to point to them to change them. A set of push buttons control the changes to be made such as erase, or move. Except for legends, no written language is used.[31]

Sketchpad was a significant step towards full pen computing, and the next hurdle was for a way of not only drawing shapes that could be recognized by the computer, but of writing words, or instructions, that the computer could identify. As a 'natural' way for humans to communicate, a computer that could interpret and act on written commands was the Holy Grail of computer scientists, but they had struggled to devise a sensitive enough method to cope with the subtle inflections of the handwritten word. In 1964, following a lengthy development programme, the Advanced Research Projects Agency (ARPA) offered the RAND Tablet – a device that could successfully read stylus movements accurately enough to allow a computer to interpret handwriting. This stylus-tablet device, also known as the

Ivan Sutherland using Sketchpad on the TX-2, 1963.

The Rand 'Grafacon' Tablet, 1964. The start of handwriting recognition technology.

'Grafacon', came at a price. A precision-made piece of specialist equipment, it cost an enormous $18,000.[32] It worked by having a very fine mesh of conductors fixed to the underneath of a writing surface, and a stylus which, attached to the mesh, could sense its position on the writing surface to within one one-hundredth of an inch. This accuracy allowed Tom Ellis at RAND to use the Grafacon along with Ivan Sutherland's Sketchpad work as the starting point for developing his GRAphic Input Language (GRAIL) method of handwriting recognition software:

> One fundamental facility of the man-computer interface is automatic recognition of appropriate symbols. The GRAIL system allows the man to print text and draw flowchart symbols naturally; the system recognizes them accurately in real-time. The recognizable symbol set includes the upper-case English alphabet, the numerals, seventeen special symbols, a scrubbing motion [a hand-drawn squiggle] used as an erasure and six flowchart symbols – circle, rectangle, triangle, trapezoid, ellipse, and lozenge.[33]

The GRAIL system developed by Ellis was not only an important development in handwriting recognition technology. As the system contained a number of innovative text-editing facilities, it formed the basis of a keyboardless word-processing program. The final piece missing from the jigsaw was a way of combining the drawing surface of the RAND Tablet with the ability to write or draw directly onto the computer screen as in the Sketchpad system.

The solution unexpectedly came from a need to digitize the results plotted on a large number of strip chart recorder printouts. Samuel Hurst was teaching at the University of Kentucky in 1969 when he met this problem, and he and Jim Parks, a graduate student, made a digitizer that would record the results in two dimensions. They did this by using two sheets of electrically conductive paper with a sheet of ordinary paper between as an insulator to create a sensor, which was placed underneath the strip chart. The two conducting sheets were connected to separate voltmeters so that a needle prick through the strip chart and sensor was recorded as an x-coordinate by one voltmeter and, independently, a y-coordinate by the other. This initial invention became a specialized piece of scientific equipment called the 'Elograph', which Hurst patented in 1972 and which formed the basis of the company Elographics.

After discussions about other possible uses and markets for the Elograph, and with funding from Siemens to cover the costs involved, Elographics undertook the development of a transparent version of the sensor (a touchscreen) that could be used over computer displays to detect the position on screen to which a user had pointed. Hurst managed to solve this problem in 1978. It was a timely development for the company, as at this point, the increasing use of computers and digital recording methods meant that the use of strip charts rapidly diminished. Without the new touchscreen product the company would not have survived. As it was, the new product was a big success, although not even Elographics themselves had any idea how successful or important a development it would turn out to be.[34]

These advances meant that all pieces of the jigsaw needed to enable the development of the tablet computer were in place by the end of the 1970s, yet it took almost a decade until the first one actually appeared. Ralph Sklarew was the first to bring together these three technologies of pen interfaces, handwriting recognition and touchscreens into a novel consumer product. His company, Linus Technologies, produced the 'Write-Top' in 1987, a portable computer with handwriting recognition, which received patents for a 'handwritten keyboardless entry computer system'. It certainly had all the capabilities of a tablet computer, although it was not termed as such

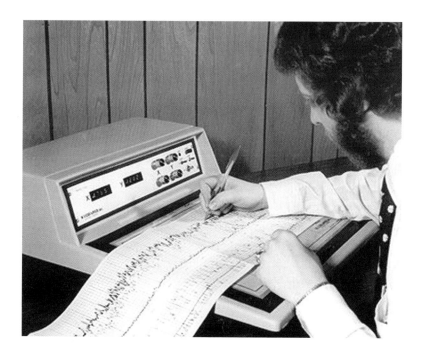

at the time. The production version (designed by Peter H. Muller of Inter4m) was a two-part design having a separate processing unit and a detachable touchscreen element connected by a cable. The two parts could be 'latched' together to create a single unit.[35] Linus Technologies demonstrated the Write-Top to a number of interested parties, including GRiD Systems,[36] but went ahead on their own, selling approximately 1,500 units before closing in 1990.[37]

The GRiDPad, conceived by Jeff Hawkins, was the first commercially successful attempt at a self-contained tablet computer, and was produced by GRiD Systems, the company that launched the GRiD 'Compass' onto the market in 1982. Sat in the offices of his new venture, Numenta, where he is developing new types of computing technology based on the workings of the human brain, Hawkins described how he had an idea for a tablet computer with a stylus-operated interface in 1987, while studying neuroscience at UC Berkeley. During a neural

Elograph Strip Chart Recorder, 1973.

networking conference, he saw a demonstration of handwriting recognition software based on pattern recognition algorithms by a company called Nestor. Hawkins realized that this could be used effectively in a mobile computer. In the autumn of 1987 Hawkins went to see GO Corporation, a promising start-up company, to see if this was a suitable place to develop the idea, but the company saw itself very much as a pen-computing business, which concerned him. In Hawkins's view, 'there's no such thing as a "pen-computing" business – you just need a PC with an additional stylus. You don't have "mouse computing" as a core business. The point is mobile computing, not pen computing.' The views of GO Corporation convinced Hawkins that they would fail as a venture. Instead, he took the idea to GRiD Systems, the company he had previously worked for, and managed the project himself. Hawkins deliberately targeted the GRiDPad at specialist, vertical markets such as insurance field workers and the medical profession because this is where he saw the best market opportunities. During 1988 he employed IDEO to work on the design of the product, and the

Linus 'Write-Top', 1987. Tablet computers were seen by the computing industry as the future product all users would want.

GRiD Systems 'GRiDPad', 1989.

simple interface the design team developed was specifically intended to aid the filling in of forms rather than inputting complex text commands. It proved to be a successful approach:

> I never saw pen computers as a replacement for a full PC as GO did. GO was really pushing pens – they lost all sense of reality. They never shipped, whereas the GRiDPad turned over in excess of $30 million in its best year.[38]

The GO Corporation Hawkins had visited was the result of a 'religious epiphany'.[39] During a flight to a business meeting in August 1987, Jerry Kaplan and Mitchell Kapor (founder of Lotus Development Corporation) discussed the potential of a portable pen-driven computer to solve all of the information-handling problems encountered by travelling executives. The GO Computer arising from this 'epiphany' was developed to the stage of a working prototype by the following year, but despite the enthusiastic support of IBM and AT&T, and significant investment by venture capitalists to the tune of $75 million, it met one engineering setback after another. A working pre-production version was finally assembled in June 1989, and a final product, with industrial design work by Paul Bradley of Matrix Design and mechanical engineering by David Kelly Design (both later to become IDEO) was completed in 1991. A development period of nearly four years for any technological product is a long time, and by the time the company had a product to sell, the partners had changed direction and decided instead to concentrate all their efforts on selling the new handwriting recognition interface software they had developed, called PenPoint. Despite the time, effort and money put into its design and development, the GO Computer was dropped without ever being offered for sale. Their move into software put GO Corporation into direct competition with Microsoft and their

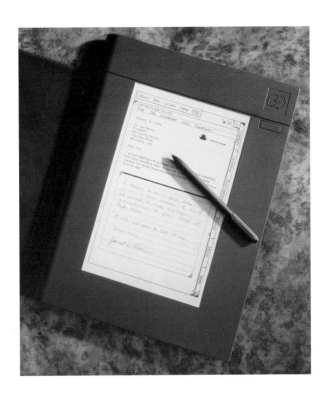

'Windows for Pen Computing' program and resulted in a court case, which perhaps unsurprisingly, GO Corporation lost. Hawkins's view of the company's potential had been prophetic. Kaplan went on to write an autobiography in which he said: 'The real question is not why the project died, but why it survived as long as it did with no meaningful sales.'[40] GO Corporation was quietly taken over by one of its financial supporters, AT&T, in 1994, and eventually shut down.

Another radical pen-computing product that at least did make it to market, even if only for a short time, was the Momenta Pentop computer of 1991. Like GO Corporation, the founder of Momenta International, Kamran Elahian, thought that the perfect pen-computing

GO Computer prototype, 1991.

operating system was just waiting to be created. Consequently, the Pentop had its own unique Graphical User Interface that represented 'yet another effort to define the look and feel of pen computing'.[41] Critics had severe reservations about yet another interface entering the market being confusing for consumers.

The target market for the Momenta Pentop also seemed confused. Tablet computers such as the GRiDPad had established a market with specialist field workers who used paperwork in a particular way, filling in a lot of forms. In contrast, the Pentop was aimed at mobile executives, and surprisingly the handwriting recognition function was played down. Instead, Momenta saw the pen and their new graphical interface as a more intuitive alternative to the mouse. This confusion in an untested market meant that despite the Momenta Pentop having many innovative features and receiving wide media coverage, the product made little impact. Momenta International ceased trading less than a year after the product's launch. Reflecting on his career in *Fast*

Momenta Pentop, 1991.

Company magazine, Elahian said: 'We set out to create a computer that would be incredibly easy to use. I was absolutely convinced that we would revolutionize the PC industry.' The same article concluded: 'There was just one problem. No one bothered to build a market for pen-based computers . . . Momenta was a monumental flop.'[42]

Other established manufacturers invested heavily in developing tablet computers around this time, but most did not see the light of day. IBM announced the imminent launch of a keyboardless tablet computer in 1992, using the operating system developed by GO Corporation.[43] However, by the time the product actually reached the market it had become a range of high-quality, sleek but standard laptops with industrial design work by Richard Sapper and Kazuhiko Yamazaki. Only the name of the prototype, 'ThinkPad', remained. Apple ran a whole series of projects with some of the best known names in the industrial design field throughout the late 1980s and early 1990s to develop tablet computers, most of which were cancelled.[44] These included a notebook-sized, slate-type computer concept codenamed 'Figaro' between 1987 and 1991 (which evolved into the Newton), the PenMac, the Macintosh Folio and SketchPad, all in 1992; and the WorkCase and Newton MessageSlate in 1993.

A spin-off company from GO Corporation called EO Inc. did have some success in 1993 with two interesting versions of tablet computers called 'Personal Communicators'. Hartmut Esslinger and his team at Frog Design carried out the industrial design work for these units, while the engineering was done in-house under Celeste Baranski. The communicators were technically quite advanced, having built-in modems to provide phone, fax and electronic mail capabilities. The smaller-screened version, the EO 440, was well received, selling around 10,000 units, but the company collapsed shortly after launching the larger-screened EO 880 and, like its parent company, it was sold off to AT&T.[45]

Even Jeff Hawkins admitted he struggled to follow his success with the GRiDPad. His idea for the GRiD Convertible computer combined the best features of laptop and tablet computers. It looked like a standard laptop, but used a clever mechanism by the industrial design team at IDEO, which allowed the screen to slide and pivot to cover the keyboard, converting it from a laptop into a tablet computer format. Hawkins said that when it was launched in 1993, 'Bill Gates loved it. It failed in the market place. I learned at that time that people didn't really want to write on their display.'[46] He realized that 'people wouldn't pay for or compromise the quality of a laptop for a pen interface.'[47]

Apple PenMac Hand-held Computer Concept, 1992.

After years of effort, major financial investments and a string of innovations, product after promising product failed to be accepted by customers. Despite the gold rush by manufacturers to launch new machines, the market for tablet computers just simply wasn't there. Pen computing appeared to be another of the industry's unfulfilled dreams. Reflecting on the state of the industry in 1994, the Editor of *Pen Computing Magazine* wrote:

> To say that the pen computing industry was struggling was a vast understatement. 'Dying,' 'reviled,' 'ridiculed' would more aptly describe it.[48]

But the dream refused to die. The poor response to Hawkins's GRiD-Pad and the demise of its various predecessors were not enough to

GRiD Convertible, 1993.

stop manufacturers from trying to turn Kay's visionary 'Dynabook' concept into reality. IBM intermittently refloated the tablet idea – firstly in prototypes of an 'Advanced Tablet' with communications functions, and in 2001 with the TransNote, a $3,000 ThinkPad with a real paper pad at its side placed over a sensor that could transfer handwriting and sketches to a text file in the same way as the RAND Tablet. It lasted a year in production before being dropped. Sony produced a desktop computer with a touchscreen called the 'Slim-top Pen Tablet PC' in 2001, but it too was discontinued due to low sales only a year later.[49] Intel presented its 'Florence' Tablet concept prototype in 2003. Lenovo (the Chinese company that bought the 'ThinkPad' brand in 2005) launched the ThinkPad X Series Tablet, which is still in production, and HP, Dell and others still produce a variety of models. Despite their low sales, manufacturers remain convinced of the potential of tablet computers. Bill Gates for one openly defends them; predicting they soon will come into their own as products, and ensuring that the latest versions of the 'Windows' operating system support pen computing.

However 'natural' a form of communication writing may appear to be, a pen writing on a display screen is not the best user interface for

IBM TransNote, 2001.

a computer. The feel of pen on paper is a difficult one to surpass, and handwriting recognition technology still isn't good enough or easy enough to use. According to Stuart Card, a research scientist at Palo Alto Research Center and an expert in human/computer interaction, the problem of pen computing is self-evident, and revolves around the difficulty of overcoming the physical keyboard:

> The reason pen computing doesn't work well is that the software it works with was designed to be used with a mouse and keyboard – the pen input was added later. PenPoint [the operating system developed by GO Corporation] was better as it was gesture-based . . . The pen clearly has an advantage if the input is a drawing, but how many people use that? And virtual keyboards are useless for typing – only one key at a time. You will always need a keyboard for bulk text input.[50]

Additionally, the complexity of a personal computer, which is accepted in a desktop PC, makes using a tablet computer difficult. The PC's slow start-up and large size and weight do not cross over well to situations in which the computer is held and carried around by the user, and constantly turned on and off. This might explain why a more specialized, handheld computer that was small, light and started instantly was so easily accepted where the tablet struggled: the Personal Digital Assistant or PDA.

Handheld Computers

The Personal Digital Assistant is actually a product quite distinct from the computer, as its primary function is to be an organizer of personal information rather than solving mathematical problems. Their design development, though, is closely related. For many years, electronic calculators had been getting more and more sophisticated, and since the mid-1970s had gradually gained extra functions such as clocks, timers and the ability to store and retrieve personal information such as memos, dates and appointments. By the end of the 1970s, alphanumeric input was a common feature on more expensive calculators. These developments culminated in hybrid products such as Toshiba's 1978 'Memo Note 30' calculator (which was primarily a calculator with memo functions), and later the Psion Organiser of 1984 (which was primarily an organizer with calculating functions). Such products were limited in use, though, by their small liquid crystal display screens and their inability to synchronize in any way with other computers. They appear now as confused artefacts – almost making sense but managing somehow to miss the point.

Apple got the point. The development work that Apple had been carrying out on tablet computers throughout the late 1980s and early 1990s ran into trouble when Apple decided that such a product might detract attention and sales from the Macintosh computer. Instead, the project was refocused as a Personal Digital Assistant, bringing a new product category into play.[51] The Apple Newton MessagePad was first announced in May 1992 at the Consumer Electronics Show, where in typical Apple style, it was heralded as the 'future of computing'. When it was finally shipped the following year, its poor handwriting recognition functionality, large size and high cost caused it to receive weak reviews. A number of redesigns were produced, eventually culminating in 1997 in the MessagePad 2000, at which point the technology was placed into the Apple eMate laptop computer and then dropped altogether a year later. The Newton was produced for six years and won various design awards, but it was never the success Apple had hoped for. It didn't 'reinvent personal computing', but it did define the product type for future developments.

The real success story of the Personal Digital Assistant is that of Palm, founded in California by the same Jeff Hawkins that was behind

the GRiDPad tablet computer. When observing people using the GRiD-Pad and talking to them, he realized that the fact that the GRiDPad turned on instantly was a major attraction and the main feature that distinguished it from a normal computer. Users really liked the simplicity of the touch-sensitive interface and also told him they would like to store their own, personal information on it. Hawkins realized that users would appreciate a smaller, lighter product with the same feeling of intimacy and accessibility of the GRiDPad.[52] On founding Palm Software in 1992, their first attempt at such a product (the Zoomer, manufactured by Casio in 1993) was approached as if they

Apple Newton MessagePad 100, 1993. Apple's attempt to 'reinvent personal computing'.

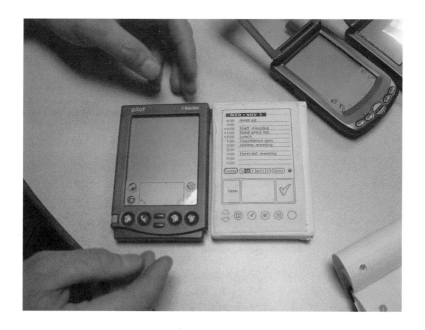

were designing a computer and as a result, it did not succeed. At this point, Hawkins was inspired by a small but complex to use Sony product that had Japanese character handwriting recognition. 'When I saw the Sony Pen Top that's when I got the idea for the Palm Pilot actually . . . I said to myself there's a consumer market here.'[53] When his team started to design the Palm Pilot, however, they realized that the use of a touch-sensitive screen meant that their competition was not the computer, but a pencil and paper. The technology itself should be invisible. That single insight changed the whole development programme, and instead of worrying about computing capabilities, the design team observed people using paper-based filing systems. In their view, the product had to be easier to use and more convenient than their pen and paper counterparts, or else why would anyone buy it? To try out the interface, a small wooden block model was created

Palm Pilot 1000, 1996, alongside wooden prototype. Recognizing that the competition for the PDA was not a computer but a pencil and paper changed the direction of Palm's design development.

and post-it notes stuck on it to simulate different application interfaces. The design team role-played with the block model, pretending to write on it in meetings to take notes, input appointments or store information. If something couldn't fit on the post-it note, it was rejected; and if an action couldn't be achieved in a single step, the whole process was rethought. A huge amount of effort was put into their version of handwriting recognition software, called Graffiti, which proved to be highly functional and was later licensed to other manufacturers, including Apple. As Hawkins stated, it was 'a controversial thing because Xerox claimed [I] stole it from them'.[54] In using the Graffiti system, each letter is simplified to a different single stroke and is written in the same space on the screen, on top of the previous letter rather than from left to right as with other systems. This meant each letter could be bigger and therefore more easily transcribed by the software. The resulting product was a triumph of interface design. The Palm Pilot 1000 was launched in 1996, and featured a calendar, contact database, task list and notepad functions all operated by dedicated buttons. The unit turned on instantly, as expected, and synchronized seamlessly with a personal computer with the push of a single button on its base unit. Its ease of use made it an instant hit with users, and it raised the consumers' expectations of PDAs to such an extent that other manufacturers were forced to offer the same functionality.

So, by the middle of the 1990s, consumers had four different handheld mobile electronic computing and communication products to choose from, each focused on a different function. For the function of data processing, miniaturization had reduced the potential size of the computer to such an extent that by 1991 Hewlett-Packard were able to offer small, handheld, IBM-compatible Palmtop PCs. Mobile phones for voice communication had been on the market since the 1970s, with small, handheld consumer versions from Motorola appearing in the early 1980s. By 1996, the Nokia 9000 Communicator included

a number of personal organization functions to produce what have become known as 'smartphones'. The Personal Digital Assistant, or 'Connected Organizer' as the Palm Pilot was labelled, was ideal for the storage and organization of personal information. Palm released a 'Professional' version in 1997 which, when synchronized with a PC, could upload and store received emails. These could be dealt with and replied to, and new emails could be written while on the move but they would not be updated or sent until the unit was once again docked and synchronized with the PC. The ability to send and receive emails in real time while on the move (known as 'push email') was popularized by a different piece of equipment called the 'Blackberry', developed by the Canadian company Research in Motion (RIM). This product first appeared on the market in 1996 as a two-way paging device called the 'Inter@ctive Pager'. It had a fully functional 'qwerty' keyboard, and a trackwheel for scrolling through messages displayed on a small LCD screen. It also had some organizational functions

HP95LX Palmtop Computer, 1991.

including an address book, a calendar with alarm and a task list. By 2002, the Blackberry could also be used as a mobile phone, but its major draw remained push email. It became so synonymous with the busy executive, who found the ability to stay constantly in touch at all times so addictive, that the device's nickname of the 'Crackberry' became a part of the language.

These four discrete product groups went through a rapid process of technological convergence driven by consumer demand. The attractive simplicity of the Palm Pilot was a revelation, but was soon

Nokia 9210 Communicator, 2000.

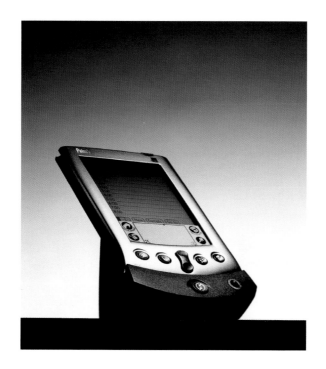

forgotten as 'feature creep' set in. PDAs gained more and more soft-ware packages in addition to their organizing functions, bringing them closer to handheld PCs. Following on from Palm, Jeff Hawkins's spin-off company, Handspring, went even further. They launched a colourful line of products in 1999 called the Handspring Visor that had an expansion slot system called 'Springboard'. Using prototype samples to demonstrate the system, into which users could plug a wide variety of plug-in modules, including modems, cameras, games modules, voice recorders and even a mobile phone module, Hawkins admitted: 'I learned that people didn't want to put a phone in their PDA, they wanted to put a PDA in their phone. Big difference. I got that wrong.'[55] Handheld PCs had basic organization applications

Palm V, 1999.

already, but these were soon improved and they also gained larger, touch-sensitive screens and handwriting recognition capabilities, bringing them closer to the functionality of PDAs. Many mobile phones used a mobile version of the Windows PC interface, and also gained numerous computing functions. Once all four products had full-colour touchscreens and wireless connectivity, there was very little to choose between them,[56] and for some years, the decision to go with one product over another became largely one of personal preference. The 2007 launch of the Apple iPhone represented the first significant attempt to seriously rethink these somewhat confused products in their entirety and sensibly combine all the features of a computer, phone, organizer, media player and web browser in one considered, well-resolved package.

The key to the usability of the iPhone lay in its use of the multi-touch screen. The first mobile device to use this technology, it allowed complex commands to be drawn with more than one finger, opening up a whole new catalogue of gesture-based operations for scrolling, zooming and rotating information, and doing away with the need for a keyboard or stylus. Although marketed primarily as a mobile

RIM 850 Inter@ctive Pager, 1996.

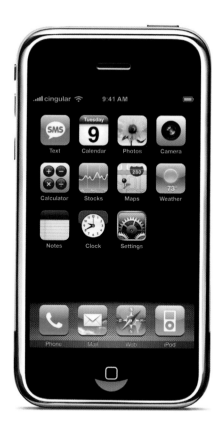

phone (possibly as it is this function that generates revenue), the iPhone is quite clearly a multi-functional computer product. The level of excitement surrounding its launch caught its competitors by surprise, and they were quick to respond with similar products. General Mobile, Dell, Sony, HTC and others formed a consortium and all produced phones based on Google's Android operating system, which gave similar application functionality to the iPhone. Jeff Hawkins's response was the Palm Pre, which sported similar touchscreen capability, a slide-out keyboard, and wireless charging through electro-magnetic induction. The computer had come a long way from the do-it-yourself attempts to 'own' computing technology.

Apple iPhone, 2007. The first serious attempt to rethink the convergence of computer, mobile phone, organizer, media player and web browser.

In the end, the change to seeing the computer as a personal object as opposed to a corporate asset happened relatively quickly. At the start of the 1970s the only personal computers available were severely limited in their functionality, and usually had to be assembled from a kit; yet by the end of the decade they had become a recognized mainstream computer product with impressive capabilities and future potential. Over the following decade, the computer became a truly portable and personal device in the form of the laptop, and by a decade later could be fitted in a pocket. In the process, a far wider group of users gained access to computing technology than ever before, and the computer was no longer the sole reserve of the world of work, but also became an exciting tool for self-development, leisure, communication and entertainment. Vannevar Bush's 1945 vision of the Memex had not only been met, but surpassed. The world of computing could finally be held in the hand.

a computer that understands your language

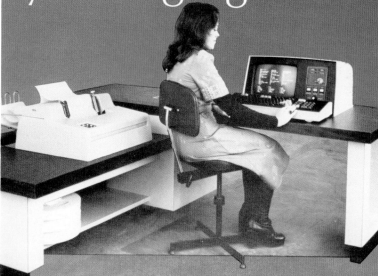

An office styled computer controlled by your staff to suit your own business needs

3 | Power Tools

'If she can type your letters, she can control our computer.' Seeing such a condescending statement in any kind of brochure today is un-thinkable, but in 1976, a computer brochure produced by Lomac Adam used these words as the USP for their latest product. Moreover, the intended operator of the computer was not even considered as being more important than the machine itself: 'Just about anywhere you'd locate a typist would be okay for LOMAC ADAM . . . Just plug into regular power and switch on.' Such innate sexism, unacceptable today, was not uncommon at the time, and was not restricted to computers, nor even to the workplace. It does appear particularly marked in this context, though, perhaps because we now expect objects that are sold primarily on their technical capabilities to be somehow neutral.

In fact, the vast majority of the visual material promoting com-puters prior to the mid-1980s clearly displays strongly gendered atti-tudes highlighting the wider socio-political agendas and stereotypical work practices of the time. In 1986 two computer historians analysed magazine adverts to assess how they reflected the perception of the computer by the public. They concluded that: 'The campaign strategy of presenting novelty within the context of the familiar means that advertising involving the office uses accepted stereotypes and rein-forces conventional views of occupational and sexual roles.'[1] As a

Brochure for Lomac Adam Computers, 1976.

new and highly expensive piece of technology brought into the office, the computer was sold to those in charge, irrespective of who would actually use it. Consequently, more than one manufacturer produced brochures depicting female office workers draped over computers in the same irrelevant way that female models were photographed alongside high-performance cars.

Closer analysis of this visual material uncovers a direct relationship between different forms of computers and the roles of their expected users. Office computers were not the homogeneous products they are today. Different computers were employed for specific purposes, and they reflected the relative level of status and power of their users. The designed forms of computers displayed physical elements specifically aligning them to stereotypically gendered roles. In one form or another, in the office, in the home or on the move, the computer played the part of a signifier of importance, a role-setting object and a lifestyle icon. Far from being meaningless, anonymous objects, they had agency. Computers were not just neutral props in the background of a sexist stage – they were instrumental actors in playing out social issues of power, control, status and gender.

Girl Power

Though seemingly remarkably sexist when viewed through the politically correct eyes of today, adverts containing text such as 'Behind the range of advanced NCR computers is an even more important product – the men whose knowledge and experience can put computers to work in your business with speed, efficiency, economy' were not intended to be contentious in any way, and did nothing but reflect the socio-political mores of the day. They come from a different world, where men were portrayed as executives, managers, scientists and engineers, while women were portrayed in subservient roles,

Muldivo's new
computer has
a very
attractive
figure...   a slim £2,425

as office juniors, secretaries, operators and assistants. Brochures depicting females using computers inevitably continued existing
practices and showed them performing typing duties or inputting
data using keyboards in exactly the same, familiar way that they
were previously presented using the traditional office typewriter. In
a similar way, when males and females were shown together in the
vicinity of computers, the familiar subordination of women to male
bosses in the office was portrayed and reinforced. Women sat at computers working away typing, while men stood watching, handing
work to them, or looked over their shoulders, checking all was well.
Such images mask a little-advertised truth. In reality, the women in
these positions had greater technological competence and more
power over these computers than their male superiors. Male managers
deliberately distanced themselves from these technologies 'lest they
be seen to be performing a "low-grade" function'.[2] Certainly, the use

Brochure for Muldivo 'Digiputer' Computers, 1968. Office computers were advertised with
models draped over them as if they were sports cars.

of computers by women was presented in the media as a low-grade role of data input, or at best secretarial support for male managers, which interestingly, reflects a dual history of the association of women with computing.

The relationship of women to the roles of word processing and of data input have separate, if related roots, depending on the equally valid views of the office computer as either a development of the typewriter or a development of the mechanical calculator. It has been well documented that women have been associated with the role of typing since the introduction of the typewriter into the office towards the end of the nineteenth century. Females were cheaper to employ to fulfil the required roles created by the huge increase in demand for office labour. Between 1861 and 1911, the number of male office clerks increased by a factor of five. In the same period, the number of female clerks increased by a factor of 500.[3] The departure of men into the armed forces during the First World War only served to fuel this expansion and consolidate typing as a feminine activity.

Similarly, despite the fact that a number of celebrated females played a key role in the early development of computing technology,[4] women were more usually associated with the low-level activity of inputting computer data. The Electronic Numerical Integrator and Computer (ENIAC) developed at the University of Pennsylvania and completed in 1946 was constructed in order to relieve a bottleneck in the production of military ballistics information during the Second World War. This clerical role was previously performed using desk-top mechanical calculators and, like typing in the office, was seen as a suitable activity for well-educated women to carry out. At one point, the US Military employed 'more than 100 female students to carry out firing table calculations'.[5] Input data for the ENIAC was fed into the machine via punched computer cards using an IBM card reader,

olivetti DE 520

The Mael 4000 business computer system.
Accurate, instant management information without the need for computer experts.

ICL Text 25, 1982.

Olivetti DE 520, 1976. Computers used by female operators were advertised as an extension of the office typewriter.

NCR 8100 Series, 1978. Male managers tended to distance themselves from the operation of computers as it was seen as a low-grade job.

Computer Ancillaries Ltd Mael 4000, 1977.

"SEE, YOU CAN PROGRAM THE E101"

and the practice of preparing those cards with card punches was transferred to, and therefore became associated with, the female workforce already in place.

Thus, when they arrived in the workplace, computers were already charged with socio-political overtones, and the functions of computers designed specifically for word processing and for data input had socially constructed reasons to look markedly different to computers that were designed for providing management information.

Early office computer terminals quickly appropriated the semiology of the office desk and typewriter, and the explicit use of these forms framed their operation as a feminine activity. Office computers were used to automate and streamline many monotonous standard business procedures, such as invoicing, accounting, payroll and record keeping, and women operated and programmed those computers 'at a time when those activities were considered mundane . . . tedious and

Burroughs E101, 1955. As soon as they appeared in the office, computers took the form of office desks and typewriters.

General purpose commercial minicomputer

LogAbax

repetitive'.[6] Computers did not start to be commonly used for word processing until well into the 1970s, and when such systems did appear, they continued to emulate the typewriter in order to provide a level of continuity and familiarity for typists. In many respects, they were designed with female operators in mind, as they 'brought electronic technologies to the typewriting task, rather than taking text production technologies to the computing activity'.[7] The view that 'the processing of text was, of course, "women's work"'[8] held sway, and the relationship between the typewriter and the office computer meant that women's skills became labelled as non-technical and therefore undervalued. This issue of technical competence has been seen as being central to the 'sexual and class politics of technological work' because it conferred 'potential or actual power'.[9]

Office computers intended for clerical work continued to appear as little more than futuristic typewriters throughout the 1970s, and

LogAbax LX2500 Minicomputer, 1977.

manufacturers' brochures carried images of large groups of female operators that appeared little different to photographs of the typing pools of an Edwardian office; each operator reduced in significance by identical repetition, slaving away, inputting text or data. As a result, the association of office computers with female operatives was reinforced and normalized to the extent that a 1977 brochure advertising training for operators could justify stating: 'Consider the data preparation area of a computer project. This is almost certainly staffed by young and frequently inexperienced girls.'[10]

Not all computers in the office were used purely for clerical work. Managers did use computers although for very different reasons. Unlike today, however, computers used for these different functions, particularly from the mid-1970s to the mid-1980s, were specially designed and marketed in clearly different ways. Computers designed to be used for data input or word processing stressed the keyboard element of their design over that of the monitor, and were deliberately visually aligned with the typewriter. Occasionally, the keyboard

CDC Cyberdata Key Entry System, 1975.

Kenrick & Jefferson MDS 9000 Data Entry System, 1977.

IBM 3740 Data Entry System, 1976.

GEC Datacom 30 Viewdata Business Terminal, 1978.

even formed an integral part of the desk surface itself, tying the typing function permanently to the form of the secretarial desk. These computers were marketed as 'Data Systems', 'Data Entry Systems' or 'Data Entry Terminals' and given names such as 'Datapoint', or were termed 'Key Edit' or 'Key Entry Systems'. In contrast, attempts were made to differentiate computers specifically designed for executive use from machines designed for clerical work through their physical appearance and their nomenclature. One brochure even advertised a white plastic-cased computer as being for 'Data Entry' by the workforce, and exactly the same computer in a walnut finish for 'Data Inquiry' by the management! Management terminals more usually emphasized the monitor elements of their design, prioritizing the screen output of information over the keyed input of data. They bore names such as 'Data Screen' or 'Viewdata', but they struggled to find a relevant stylistic reference point that would distinguish them clearly from 'feminine' office workers' computers. *Design* magazine in 1981 featured a new computer designed specifically for executives that attempted to counter this problem. The author stated:

> Ergonomically optimised for long periods of key bashing by specialist operation, computer terminals aren't usually suited to use by company executives. What's more, rather than building up a desirable space-age corporate commander image, most of them look likely to lower a manager's status to that of the lowly VDU worker with managerial pretensions.[11]

The technological appearance of the QED MT-02 was intended to express 'sophisticated engineering', and it used advanced electronics to enable the keyboard to 'talk' to the monitor via an infra-red transmitter. The sharp, clean and precisely detailed styling of the terminal

casing deliberately aimed to endow the computer with the same executive and masculine connotations as a finely engineered watch or camera.

The activities of managers were perhaps less tangible and more difficult to relate to particular physical forms, which may go some way to explaining the expansion of the role of 'masculine' office computers and the appearance of confused objects such as the computer as telephone or computer as intercom. Such devices were blatant attempts to indicate status in the workplace, and the ability of the office computer to act as a status symbol requires some clarification. Usually, for an object to work as a status symbol, there has to be a recognized monetary value the owner has expended, and it is this recognized value that is translated into a symbolic value of the owner's status. However, in the case of the office computer no personal economic investment has been made, merely an investment by the company, and the computer is therefore weakened as a status symbol. What status there is comes from the company's selection of who is and who is not provided with such 'executive' objects. It is an endorsement of status by superiors, which may or may not be permanent.

QED MT-02, 1981. A computer terminal designed for executive use.

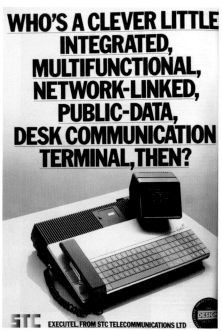

WHO'S A CLEVER LITTLE INTEGRATED, MULTIFUNCTIONAL, NETWORK-LINKED, PUBLIC-DATA, DESK COMMUNICATION TERMINAL, THEN?

STC EXECUTEL. FROM STC TELECOMMUNICATIONS LTD

Expected masculine behaviour also perhaps explains the text and imagery in brochures of computers aimed at male managers having a markedly different bias from those intended for clerical work. The business benefits of the computer were sold explicitly, stressing the strong performance, how versatile and adaptable the machines were, and how 'effective'. The brochure for the Racal-Redac 'Redac Executive' stated: 'Individual video display units are provided for the managing director, production director/manager, financial director/chief accountant, and marketing director/manager. These units are located in the individual's own office, and are always ready for immediate use.' Moreover, the use of the term 'control' was extensive, whether it was 'production control', 'budget control' or 'record control'. These brochures, containing images of men working alone on computers, were not as common as those with images of women working alone, suggesting that although used for managerial control,

ICL One Per Desk, 1984. Computers for managerial use had no precedent of form to follow. Was it a typewriter, a telephone or an intercom?

STC Executel, 1984.

UNIVAC Uniscope 100, 1975. Male managers were not usually shown typing when using a computer, but reading, writing or speaking on the telephone.

Racal-Redac 'Redac Executive', 1977.

it was still considered as less than 'executive' for men to be seen with an object operated by typing.

The association of computers with low-level and low-status typing work accounts for the presence of a range of other objects that are almost always present in images of men working at computers throughout the 1970s and into the 1980s. To indicate their importance, distance themselves from the role of typing, and perhaps to retain their masculinity and power, men were depicted using a telephone, writing on clipboards or pads of paper, and if touching the keyboard at all, only ever using one hand to enter commands. The computer was depicted as subordinate to their need to talk and write, its role being to provide supporting information to make managerial decisions. The text of these brochures confirms that managers consulted computers to obtain forecast data, not to input information.

In addition to these socially constructed differences, technological developments throughout the late 1960s and 1970s also had a marked impact on the use of computers in the office. The advent of commercially available integrated circuits in the second half of the 1960s shrank the size of computers significantly. Computers began to appear as more human-scale products, less incomprehensible and more 'friendly' than isolated, distant mainframes. Remote computer terminals on office desks had been the only access for workers to such machines, as their requirement for an air-conditioned environment meant they were necessarily separated from the office itself. Even when mainframe computers could be seen through the glass walls of their enclaves, lowly workers were not allowed near them.[12] This was a privilege reserved only for specialists. But the continuing reductions in the size and expense of electronic components meant that computing power in the mid-1970s was roughly one hundredth of the cost of a decade earlier. Gradually, this reduced the economic arguments for timesharing computers and enabled remote terminals connected to centralized machines to finally be replaced by self-contained computers. For a while, such elite machines were only made available for professional applications in engineering or scientific research ('portable power for specialists everywhere'!),[13] but eventually appeared for general management use towards the end of the 1970s. The easier availability of smaller magnetic storage devices also led to many computer terminals and workstations acquiring archiving capabilities on removable media such as cassettes or disks. Predictably, the main impact of this was to turn the computer into an electronic filing cabinet as well as an electronic typewriter, and only served to reinforce its association with low-grade, female clerical work. Obviously aware of this standing and hence the morale of its users, the manufacturers of the Kode DataVet presented computer storage capabilities as a way of expanding the appeal of the computer operator's role. Somewhat unconvincingly, their brochure stated: 'DataVet keystations are designed to reduce the keying workload and motivate the operators, the tangible end product – a cassette – helps each operator to feel involved and of value.'[14]

Nixdorf 8820, 1977.

Kode DataVet Keystation, 1976.

Yet despite these various technological developments, the provision of significantly different computers performing discrete roles for different divisions of the office remained in place well into the 1980s, even following the launch of the IBM PC in 1981. From this point, desktop computers became widely known as 'personal computers', and became a more common element of office topography. Yet regardless of their multi-functional capabilities and their potential value to management, they and their clones were still usually shown being used by female secretaries for the increasingly popular application of word processing. Changes in the representation of office computers in manufacturers' literature that were indicative of wider social changes slowly appeared as the decade progressed. The 1980s saw a marked increase in sexual equality in the workplace, as attitudes instigated and reinforced through legislation took hold.[15] These social and legislative changes gradually reduced the distinction between male and female roles, and the depiction of women undertaking menial roles in the office and men holding positions of

ICL Personal Computer Model 30, 1982.

IBM System/36 'Team Computer', 1987. It finally became acceptable for males to use the same computers as females towards the end of the 1980s.

authority became less evident. By the mid- to late 1980s men and women started to be shown using the computer together as equal members of a team.

Nevertheless, a noticeable change from the production of different computers for workers and management only occurred at the start of the 1990s. This was when the impact of the Graphical User Interface and the computer mouse really started to be felt in the workplace, although why they should have become so popular in the office environment in the first place is not as obvious as one might think. The cost of computing technology, although constantly reducing, was still high enough that by far the largest market for 'personal computers' was in business – and in business, skilled female typists operated the vast majority of the installed base of computers. The widespread use and momentum of text-based software, operated in a manner so closely related to the typewriter, should have theoretically made the adoption of an unfamiliar, visually based, icon-driven system very difficult. Certainly, it is quite clear from the literature supplied with the first Apple Macintosh machines and from third-party texts that the introduction of the mouse was a huge change for existing computer users. The first manuals for the Macintosh devoted entire sections on how to use them, reassuringly stating: 'Using the mouse might feel a little awkward at first, but it will soon be second nature';[16] and: 'If you can point, you can use a Macintosh.' Whole books were written to convince Mac owners of the benefits of using a mouse:

> If you're like most people, you're probably muttering one (or more) of the following complaints about mice: 'Mice are stupid; they slow things down'; 'My desk is too small and crowded to make room for a mouse'; and 'You have to take your hand off the keyboard to use the mouse.' A fair warning: Don't be quick to condemn the Mac's mouse before you've tried it – *really* tried it.[17]

But using a mouse with a Macintosh that had a graphical interface specifically designed to be used with a mouse was a very different story to using a mouse with a PC. Mice had been available for use with the IBM PC since Microsoft produced one in 1983, but they failed to have any impact as the only operating system they could be used with was the text-based MS-DOS (Microsoft Disc Operating System). This is not surprising considering that the expected practice was for users to write their own mouse menus for existing programs using software provided. When Microsoft launched their copy of the Macintosh interface, 'Windows 1.0', in 1985, they even incorporated free programs to help people become familiar with using mice. These included Notepad, a mouse-based text editor, Piano, an on-screen piano keyboard that could be 'played' with the mouse, and later a simple mouse-operated drawing program called Doodle, but to no avail. Early versions of the Windows operating system were slow and clunky as IBM PCs were just not designed to handle graphics. After five years on the market, mice were still only used on less than ten per cent of all PCs.[18] This state of affairs changed drastically when a viable version of a graphical interface for PCs – 'Windows 3.0' – became available in 1990.

Of course, what the GUI and the computer mouse did achieve was to allow the association of the computer with the typewriter to disappear altogether. No matter how powerful or how small word-processing computers had become, they were operated purely by typing and remained associated with female operators. Computers designed for managerial work, as we have seen, struggled to differentiate themselves from workers' computers, and their use by male managers remained problematic. With the introduction of the GUI and the mouse, this problem disappeared altogether. The office computer could now be perceived as a completely new piece of technology that could acceptably be used by both female office workers and male managers as it was operated in a totally different way. The computer with a mouse was suddenly a new, multi-functional device that had broken free of its predecessors and had no specific association with a particular gender. Although it did not completely remove the need for a keyboard, the use of a computer mouse was empowering. It allowed the direct manipulation of information with one hand only. Rather than 'type' or 'input', the relevant words became 'point', 'click', 'drag' and 'drop' – the very terminology of command and control. It was the computer mouse, not equality legislation, that allowed a single form of office computer to take hold.

In addition to losing its gender associations as it became a single product used by all, the office computer lost its ability to infer status. Theories of status and emulation[19] rely on 'reciprocal differentiation' – in which there is a constant move to a new position by a superordinate group, providing a new target to be achieved by a subordinate group. The ability of the new, singular office computer to function as a role-setting object or a status symbol was effectively removed by the fact that any of the now identical machines could be running any software. A male or female using a computer in an office could be either a secretary using a word-processing package or a financial director using budgeting software. It was no longer possible to distinguish between the two using the computer as an indicator, as it had now become a completely 'natural' and neutral part of the office environment.

Toys for the Boys I – Home Computers

Ironically, while the vast majority of computers in the male-dominated environment of the office happened to be controlled by women, computers in the home were almost exclusively the reserve of men. Here, they functioned far less readily as status symbols or role-setting

objects than their office counterparts as they were more private goods, seen only by immediate family and friends. Their use, however, like many other domestic technologies, was heavily gendered. Stereotypically gendered roles were, of course, as common in representations of domestic environments as they were in representations of work environments. It comes as no surprise then, that images and writings about early home computers displayed similarly sexist attitudes to those in brochures for office computers. An early article on the potential of computing in the home in a 1970 issue of *Life* magazine related the story of Dr Rodman, a specialist at Temple University medical school in Philadelphia, who brought home a Teletype terminal connected through a telephone line to a timesharing mainframe computer 90 miles (145 km) away in New Jersey. The intention was to use the terminal to be able to carry out medical research while spending more time with his family, 'but then his family found it could also plan mortgage payments, help out with homework, even play with the children'.[20] The images accompanying the article showed the

Early adopters: the Rodman family with their Teletype computer terminal, 1970.

males of the household programming the computer to achieve a whole variety of tasks, including a program to generate weekly meal menus, while Mrs Rodman (despite being a career woman in her own right) settled for using a computer-generated shopping list in the local store and making use of computer print-out paper as an alternative to gift-wrap![21] Similarly, in 1977, a very telling pair of images appeared advertising the Apple II computer. A sales brochure showed the computer being used in the home by a happy couple to play computer games together. Yet in *Scientific American* magazine a few months later, the same couple were shown in an advert where the Apple II was being used for the 'serious' work of checking the Dow Jones Index. Here, it was operated solely by the male, while the female of the household was shown undertaking a stereotypically feminine domestic role of preparing a meal.

The association of home computing with male users lies with its origins being so different to computing in the office. The office

Homebrew Computer Club newsletter no. 2, April 1975.

People's Computer Company Newsletter no. 1, October 1972.

computer was initially developed from scientific research equipment, which over time became information-processing machinery used for carrying out everyday business procedures. As such, it was a product of the establishment, and their use was largely associated with female operators. In contrast, the home computer (which has now arguably disappeared as a discrete product type) had its roots in male hobbyist activities as an extension or development of the pastimes of do-it-yourself radio enthusiasts and electronics devotees. Women's views of such pastimes are not always complimentary:

> In general male hobbies can be distinguished from female hobbies in that the latter need little capital outlay and have a useful end-product (they are often related to pre-industrial crafts), such as knitting, sewing, embroidery, even flower-arranging, whereas the former need a large capital outlay and produce little or no end product, being done for the pleasure of the activity itself, for example, fishing, photography, ham radio and electronics.[22]

Unfortunately, exactly how 'useful' flower arranging is is not clarified. Similarly questionable is the view that male-oriented do-it-yourself activities provide no useful end product, particularly in the areas of ham radio and electronics. The magazines supporting these practices were (and still are) largely based around practical projects to produce functional goods and devices (irrelevant of their standard of finish). Yet, the home computer in the early 1970s was far removed from the office computer of the same period. They were not attractively designed objects – a typical home computer was a mysterious small steel box covered in switches, lights and buttons – and it has to be admitted that they were used for little else other than experimental programming. There was a direct lineage from male hobbyists involved in the construction of electronics projects who gave up their old interests to become 'immersed in the world of microcomputing', and the take up of the microcomputer by 'early [male] adopters . . . helped to give the home-based machine its "masculine" image'.[23]

These hobbyists, as well as communicating through specialist magazines and self-published newsletters, gathered together outside the home to discuss their interests with other like-minded enthusiasts at male-dominated computer societies and self-help clubs. The most famous of these were based in San Francisco: The People's Computer Company of the early 1970s and its later spin-off, the Homebrew Computer Club of 1975. Both of these not only acted as meeting points but also had the (then rather subversive) aim of bringing computer technology within reach of the average person. The association of the Apple computer to the Homebrew Computer Club is the reason for that particular group being considered one of the two birthplaces of personal computing (the other being Xerox PARC, where the Graphical User Interface was developed). A number of writers have argued that the subversive, or counter-cultural attitude prevalent in San Francisco at this time was central to the development of personal computing. Its influences can be traced back to Stewart Brand's anti-establishment *Whole Earth Catalog* of 1968, and earlier to 'the extraordinary convergence of politics, culture, and technology that took place in a period of less than two decades and within the space of just a few square miles'.[24]

But a much earlier and very different type of male-dominated social network played an influential role in the development of home computing, despite its focus initially being in quite a different area. The Tech Model Railroad Club (TMRC) was founded in 1947 at the Massachusetts Institute of Technology. MIT was the home of hugely significant research work into radar during the war, as well as post-war developments into digital computing in the form of the

'Whirlwind' and 'TX-0' computers created for the American Military. In turn, these influential computers led directly to the long-serving SAGE Air Defence System for the United States Air Force and later to developments in speech and handwriting recognition, interactive computing and computer graphics.

The TMRC was based in Building 20, the old Radiation Lab where radar research had been carried out. As a 'temporary' flexible space, Building 20 ended up as the home of many of the more radical, untested programmes of study and research, bringing together a range of disparate intellectual mavericks under the same roof. Alan Kotok and Peter Samson were students at MIT in the late 1950s and early 1960s, and were active members of the TMRC. The club's model railway was already a hugely complex layout, and club members routinely scavenged components from other departments to create circuits to control the model trains. These circuits included electro-mechanical relays from research projects in advanced telephone switching systems, which were being developed for companies such as Western Electric. Using these 'unofficially' obtained parts, the club built the first control system of its kind, which would allow multiple controllers to simultaneously operate trains on different sections of the same model railway network.[25] Samson is also credited with being the first ever computer 'hacker', as he sneaked into another MIT building to break into the IBM 704 mainframe computer housed there, and used its keypunch machine to program the railway switching system.

In 1959, Kotok and Samson were among the first cohort of students on MIT's earliest course in computer programming. During their studies, they learned about the interactive research computer, the 'TX-0', that was built there. They became proficient in programming it, and wrote a number of visually based computer games for it. In 1962, with the help of others including Steve Russell and

Martin Graetz, they worked on a DEC PDP-1 computer to develop the first ever digital video game, called *SpaceWar!*[26] The *SpaceWar!* program was distributed between enthusiasts working at different universities, and inspired a lot of people to develop their own games. One of these enthusiasts, Nolan Bushnell at the University of Utah, went on to found a computer company called Syzygy in 1971 and turned the *SpaceWar!* idea into the first ever coin-operated arcade video game, *Computer Space*.

Though *SpaceWar!* had been popular with specialist computer enthusiasts, the response of the public was more restrained. *Computer Space* was a disappointing commercial flop, largely because it was a very difficult game to learn to play. Meanwhile, Ralph Baer, a television engineer working at Sanders Associates had had the idea that televisions could be used for something other than just watching TV programmes. Since 1966, he had been working on developing a 'Television Gaming Apparatus', the first version of which was so basic, it just generated two spots of light on a TV screen. The aim of the game, called *Fox and Hounds*, was for one of the spots (the hound) to chase the other spot (the fox) until it 'caught' it.[27] The spots of light became 'balls' and a whole series of computer-generated ball games were developed. The final product was launched in 1972 by Magnavox as the 'Odyssey Home Entertainment System' and was the earliest video game console. On seeing the game *Table Tennis* on this system, Bushnell realized the key to its attraction was the game's simplicity. He changed the name of his company to Atari and quickly launched the famous *Pong* coin-operated tennis arcade video game. In the first bar where it was installed, the game suddenly stopped working after a few days. On checking, it became apparent that it had been so popular with customers that the cashbox had overflowed with coins and jammed the machine.[28] Convinced by this response, Bushnell founded a whole factory to build the games and started a whole industry. Although people who had never witnessed a video game before considered this new phenomenon revolutionary, few of them realized that the concept behind *Pong* actually went back many years. In 1958 Willy Higinbotham, an employee at Brookhaven National Laboratory in New York, had developed a similar analogue computer tennis game purely in order to entertain Open Day visitors to the site who were bored by seeing a static mainframe computer![29]

Because the activities of the members of the TMRC and entrepreneurs such as Nolan Bushnell led more to games and software development than to computer hardware itself, their relevance to the development of the home computer might be easily overlooked. However, they were important in a number of ways. They had the maverick outlook often stated as the key feature of Silicon Valley entrepreneurs, and they were among the first to hijack computing technology for leisure activities, which would otherwise perhaps never have been seen as a legitimate line of development by the mainstream computer industry. The creation of games provided a popular and much sought after 'practical' application for home computers, and as CRT monitors were still relatively expensive, such video games created an alternative use for television sets, bringing the home computer out of the closet of the computer enthusiast and into the living room of the whole family. Through such use, reinforced by advertisements showing families playing video games together, the home computer became legitimized as a household product rather than an obscure hobbyist item.

Yet, despite this legitimization, it has been noted that even by the mid-1980s, 'interest in home computing remained heavily gendered, with an emerging preponderance of male teenage users'.[30] This association was reinforced by the view of early home computers at that time (certainly in Britain) as little more than machines for playing

games.[31] According to a 1983 article in the American computer magazine *Byte*, microcomputing was more popular in Britain than it was in America by some way, although those interested were 'still almost exclusively men and boys'.[32] The author explained that the British public's enthusiasm for microcomputers resulted at least in part from a government-sponsored public education programme involving the British Broadcasting Corporation, a series of television programmes and printed material, along with an 'official' microcomputer, the BBC Micro; and also in part to the 'pivotal work of one man: Clive Sinclair'.[33] The article compared Sinclair to the American Adam Osborne (creator of the Osborne 1 portable computer) as 'the creator of a product whose price is so low that the competition finally accepted it as the price to beat'.[34] Sinclair Research had launched two black and white home computers, the ZX80 and the ZX81 (in 1980 and 1981 respectively), which became 'the most popular microcomputers in Britain (and for that matter, in the rest of the world)'.[35]

Atari 'Home Computers' brochure, 1983. The use of the family television as a monitor for playing computer games brought the home computer out of the hobbyist shed.

Broader horizons

The BBC Microcomputer System

Despite this achievement, the contract to produce the BBC Micro was awarded to another British company, Acorn Computers Ltd. Sinclair went on to successfully produce his submitted design for the government-approved computer as the colour-capable ZX Spectrum in 1982, while the BBC Micro was adopted as an educational computer by the vast majority of UK schools. This should have fostered a genderless interest in home computers for applications other than game playing, but the BBC Micro was a lot more expensive than its competitors, and realizing this, its manufacturers produced a less capable, less expensive version called the Acorn Electron. The first page of the user guide stated this machine 'can be instructed to do a great variety

BBC Micro advert, 1982.

of things'[36] – playing games being the first in the list. The home computer's main use remained a male-oriented recreational one.

The phenomenon of male bias in the consumption of technology in the home has been well documented,[37] and is still present. Yet while it might be difficult today to accurately ascertain the home usage of computers by gender, it is not as male-dominated as described above – particularly amongst younger users brought up with computer technology and exposed to it as an educational tool. Even in the area of computer games, Nintendo, with the launch of the Nintendo DS and the Wii, has had a significant impact in moving the demographic of computer game users in the home to include both older users and female users. This is a recent shift, however. Only a few years ago, a book chapter titled 'Is the Home Computer Pink or Blue?' stated:

Sinclair Spectrum, 1981, with the 1983 ZX Interface 1 and ZX Microdrives.

Acorn Electron brochure, 1983.

Computers are, in many ways, still designed and manufactured in ways that exclude or discourage women and girls. Parents complain of the difficulty of finding computer games suitable for their daughters, and powerful role models for women are less visible than the stereotyped gendered representations of computer advertising.[38]

Home computers, then, were heavily gendered objects rather than status symbols. The creation of the home computer was the result of a multiplicity of disparate, yet almost exclusively male social networks operating at different times, and in very different spheres. Networks of ham radio and model railway enthusiasts with shared interests and experience in assembling electronic components for their own ends, communicating not only through the airwaves but also through self-published newsletters and professionally published specialist magazines; informal and formal social and educational networks of students and enthusiasts that nurtured programming talent in the development of gaming software; established business networks supplying electronic components, which provided a ready distribution chain for computer kits and parts at affordable prices; and, perhaps most significantly, social networks in the form of hobbyist computer clubs, whose members not only had shared interests, but shared values in that they strongly believed in easy access for all to computing technology. The home computer came from grass-roots activities mostly indulged in by men, and in many ways carried an anti-establishment attitude that removed it from any association with the office, the typewriter and its associated socio-political agendas (although it clearly developed a socio-political agenda of its own). This distance, along with the historical connection to hobbyist activity in electronics, imbued the home computer with its own aesthetic and socially constructed identity, and allowed it to move easily into the realm of being a consumer electronic product quite distinct from the office computer.

The bias of manufacturers in developing the games capability of home computers over its more 'serious' abilities meant that once the home computer had to all intents and purposes become the games console, and the office computer had become a single machine without the associations of hierarchical work roles, the office computer started to appear in the home to perform those more serious functions, further expanding its role as a 'universal' machine. Thus the home computer and the office computer became one and the same object. The only differences between the two were software related, with cheaper, 'cut-down' versions of office software appearing for home use. The office computer and the 'new' form of home computer remained indistinguishable until 1998, when Apple launched the Jonathan Ive-designed iMac.

The iMac made great play of its colourful credentials, and as the media adverts and brochures revealed, was overtly aimed at domestic users. Intended to exploit a significant increase in the use of the Internet in the home, it was sold as an 'amazingly simple' product that was 'Internet ready'. Designed to be used straight out of the box, it came with all the necessary software pre-loaded. The iMac could easily have had the effect of separating the trajectories of the home computer and the office computer once more into clearly discrete product ranges, and indeed, it did influence a number of manufacturers who launched colourful computers in wildly different forms aimed at domestic use. However, the beige box of the office computer proved a difficult precedent to change, and the majority of manufacturers stuck to what they knew. Additionally, the iMac was readily adopted in many more 'design aware' workplaces as a welcome change to the boring predictability of the universal machine, and consolidated the position of Apple computers as the products of choice by those working in the creative industries. While the iMac freed the computer from necessarily being an identical product everywhere it

appeared, the boundaries between the home computer and the office computer remained confusingly blurred.

Toys for the Boys II - Mobile Computers

In 1995, the cartoonist Scott Adams drew a *Dilbert* strip where his downtrodden computer engineer attempts to cover over his adoration for his laptop computer. Many a true word is spoken in jest, and Dilbert's love affair with the laptop is no idle joke – there is a close personal relationship evident between men and mobile computers. Historically, this relationship has understandably been very different from the relationship between users and office computers and between users and home computers. These differences stemmed largely from the status afforded by the various types of computer, which in turn was a function of the extent to which they were displayed to and seen by others. Until the mid-1980s, the form of computers in the office clearly displayed the hierarchies of their users, but they were in the main seen only by other members of the office workforce or by invited visitors to the workplace. Home computers were largely devoid of associations of status, as although they were an overt display of technical knowledge and superiority; they were seen only by the immediate family or by like-minded members of computer clubs. Mobile computers, on the other hand, were something else.

Coloured Apple iMacs, 2000.

They were from the outset an object that would be blatantly displayed, seen by anyone and everyone. They instantly said a great deal about the person carrying them, and so were deliberately intended to project a suitably high-status image that could be easily read by all.

Long before the technology became available to create a really suitable product, numerous manufacturers had clear intentions to produce portable computers. Manufacturers understood that, given the costs involved in bringing the latest advances in computing technology to

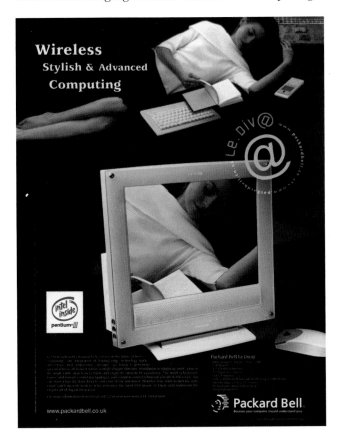

Packard Bell 'Le Div@' home computer advert, 2000.

the marketplace, such a product would have to be a business machine purchased for use by the higher echelons of the corporation. Such a customer would in any case be one of the few people who had a legitimate requirement to use a computer when not in the office. Consequently, early products in this market were aimed solely at the travelling business executive, who at that time was almost exclusively male. An expensive portable computer would not only act as a status symbol, it would also clearly indicate that its owner was travelling as a business user, and had the necessity, authority and freedom to work away from the confines of the workplace.

The difficulty facing those advertising these products was that portable computers were a completely new class of product. It could not be assumed that the reader of a brochure would understand what the product was, or the value it should carry in terms of status.[39] This is especially true as the products themselves were inside carrying cases and looked to all intents and purposes the same as large executive briefcases. Additionally, because they were deliberately intended for use outside of the office, there was no recognizable environment in which portable computers could be placed to provide a familiar context. Instead, a process of associative transference was adopted. The unique status of portable computers was projected by associating them with other objects – ones that were already understood by observers as having certain high-level qualities and attributes. By placing portable computers alongside aerial vehicles a whole series of associations were transferred from one to the other – the desirability of cutting-edge technology, the convenience of freedom of movement.

Dilbert strip by Scott Adams, 1995.

And not only were associations made between the computer and these existing objects, but their 'distinctive or superior qualities'[40] were transferred to the owner of the computer: the exclusivity of ownership, the privilege of independence and the wealth to afford the high cost of luxury. Such objects act as symbols of the self, and

Transdata 'Executive Terminal', 1974. The computer as status symbol. Executives carrying portable computer terminals were shown as 'playboy adventurers' who took a private plane or helicopter to work.

Texas Instruments 'Silent 700, Data Terminal', 1972.

'stress the unique qualities of the owner, his or her skills and superiority over others'.[41] They also act to differentiate their owners from the crowd and integrate them into a set of people sharing a similar social standing – an elite group of the higher echelons of executive life. In this process of differentiation, the potential users of portable computers were portrayed as high-flying 'world citizens'. These people were something really important, somebody really special. Not for them the mundanity of a mere car – these people travelled to work by private aeroplane or helicopter.

Such integrated groups of users have nothing to do with existing class structures – the status of the group is 'bought with products, not with money'.[42] The process is, however, a very subtle one. Customers do not just buy these products in order to become a part of the group they represent. They must already feel as though they naturally belong to such a group and will therefore buy the product in order to display such belonging. It is not so much the product itself that is the attraction to owners, but 'the self-illusory experiences which they construct from their associated meanings . . . the imaginative pleasure-seeking to which the product image lends itself'.[43]

In the case of the executive 'world citizens' in their private aeroplanes and helicopters, this 'imaginative pleasure-seeking' stemmed from popular culture and its distinctive representation of masculinity in the increasingly technological world of the 1960s and 1970s. The self-image of the male and his relationship to technology and society were underlying themes of films and television programmes at this time on both sides of the Atlantic. The particularly pervasive persona of James Bond and his latest gadgets, along with other male role models such as Simon Templar in *The Saint*, Steed in *The Avengers*, Napoleon Solo and Illya Kuryakin in *The Man from U.N.C.L.E.*, and Jim Phelps in *Mission: Impossible*, all played an important role in redefining masculine identity and its associated expectations of technological competence. These men were agents for an 'upwardly mobile jet-set', encapsulating a lifestyle promoted through the increased advertising and consumption of the time. Breaking the shackles of office boredom, they moved in a 'mythologized world of hedonism, consumer pleasure and individual autonomy'.[44]

These images of early portable computer users provided escapism through the promise of adventure – a life to be lived away from the drudgery of the desk. The truth of the situation, though, was somewhat different. As can be seen from closer examination of the images, 'portable data terminals' were not as portable as might be hoped. The Texas Instruments 'Silent 700' terminal, for example, was sold as being particularly lightweight for the period, weighing 'only' 13 lbs (nearly 6 kg), and that was just for a terminal without any power source or memory of its own. By way of comparison, a laptop weighing less than half of this would be considered 'heavy' by today's standards, yet would be fully self-contained and powered. Products such as the Osborne 1 were only used as portable computers under duress, and as soon as a more suitable alternative appeared, 'luggable' computers were exposed as a completely unsuitable product type and vanished almost overnight. The technology of portable computing, advanced though it was, was not enough on its own to secure acceptance among the target market of mobile executives. In order to succeed as a product, the physical form of mobile computing had to reflect the 'high technology' fashions of the 1970s, and in particular the glamorous image of masculinity emerging from the notion of the 'playboy adventurer'. Through displaying ownership of a mobile computer, owners had to be able to present themselves as an upwardly mobile climber of the corporate ladder. Consequently, the image of portable technology promising a 'James Bond' lifestyle of independent freedom was a strong and clearly attractive one. Numerous manufacturers strove to create a suitably high-status portable computer that could fulfil this promise. The 'Compass' Portable Computer by GRiD, relabelled as a 'Briefcase Computer' in promotional material, was the first product to achieve this. By utilizing the very latest advances in computing technology, GRiD produced a portable computer that was highly desirable as well as highly functional, fitted easily inside a standard briefcase and was a duly fashionable signifier of executive status. Portable computers never really took off until they took this 'executive briefcase' form, and the clamshell design of the 'Compass' computer quickly became the norm for the whole industry. Where other product types had singularly failed to project the image of a 'playboy adventurer', the laptop succeeded.

The blatant signification used to promote early portable computers is quite understandable in retrospect, as a market for the product still had to be nurtured and developed. As portable computers started to become more commonplace and more easily recognized as such, the requirement for associative imagery to connote their status was reduced. Brochures for laptops in the 1990s, for example, showed the computers on plain backgrounds. The associated text didn't sell the benefits of owning such a machine as the benefits were well-known. Instead, they merely described the technical specification of the particular model shown. As the laptop became more of a mainstream product, its familiarity and popularity meant that its ability to act as a status symbol became diluted. As with the depiction of office computers, gender also became less of an issue. Adverts and brochures began to show women using laptops, although still nowhere near to the extent that they showed male users. If brochures showed both sexes using mobile computers, the male was usually shown on the front cover of the brochure and the female hidden away inside.

The self-image and body language of the use of mobile technological products was a far more significant element in their success or failure than has previously been acknowledged. The semantic associations of the use of the laptop as described above, for example, were far more in tune with the role-setting expectations of the product than were the associations of operating, for example, the military field radio-like Osborne 1. A red-faced, sweating executive struggling to carry such a thing would have impressed no one, and it is no surprise that they were very quickly dropped. The proposed successor to the laptop, the tablet computer, had a similarly problematic issue. These devices were widely lauded by the computing industry as the products of the future, but the relevant users just did not accept them. In essence a large touch-sensitive panel, tablet computers tended to be carried in the cradle of one arm, and written upon with the remaining free hand. As such, they bore a remarkable resemblance to that stalwart of bureaucracy, the clipboard. This was not so much of a problem when the products were more rugged and aimed at field workers in the insurance industry, where the clipboard was a commonly used and readily accepted piece of equipment. But when the same product type was aimed at an executive audience the result was absolutely disastrous. The clipboard has been called 'the Power Plank', its visual prominence the main reason it acted so strongly as a hierarchical marker and as 'an essential means of enforcing the strict social structure'[45] of various institutions. It could not be hidden away, and so carrying one instantly betrayed the owner's limited role and jumped-up status. Male executives should have seen the fact that tablet computers didn't have to be typed on as a benefit, as until the 1990s typing was still considered to be a feminine activity, but it seems that the requirement to write with a stylus on a glass screen was not popular. This might have been due to purely technical issues, such as the 'feel' of writing on glass compared to paper, or problems with efficacy of the interface software itself. But it might just as easily have been the case that carrying these products and

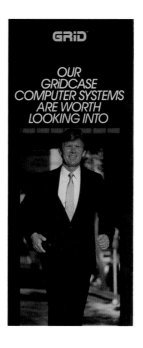

writing on them semantically associated the owner with the less than executive role of completing pro-forma questionnaires and ticking off checklists. Even the 'obvious' advantages of such a product in business meetings where they could be quietly written on rather than noisily typed on[46] does not detract from the fact that executives might have thought that they should not be the one being seen to take minutes. Although they remain in production as niche products, tablet computers clearly failed (and still fail) to portray a suitably fashionable self-image for the executive user. Yet they do seem to be more readily accepted in other markets such as healthcare and for educational use, where status is not so much of an issue. Only time will tell if Apple's new iPad tablet computer changes this position and finally breaks this elusive market.

Brochure for Osborne 'Personal Business Computer', 1981.

Brochure for GRiDCase Computers, 1985.

The technology contained within the tablet computer was transferred fairly easily to far smaller, handheld personal digital assistants. These were accepted far more readily than tablet computers ever were and were much more successful, quickly spawning an industry all of their own.[47] Specialized devices such as the Palm Pilot and the Blackberry were less traditional computers than devices aimed specifically at time management, personal data organization and communication, and as such could have had far less in the way of gender associations, yet even here gender bias was still evident. By 1997, the language used in the brochure for Apple's later version of the Newton, the MessagePad 2000, was more politically correct, stating that the product was aimed at 'anyone who spends time away from their desk',[48] but tellingly, all the images still depicted the device being used by males in business suits. The size of the product was obviously part of its appeal, and being seen to write on a discreet handheld object resembling a reporter's notepad was clearly far more acceptable than writing on a large object resembling a clipboard.

So, the desire by executive business users to project a suitably exclusive self-image through the use of technological products as role-setting objects and status symbols was a significant factor in the success or failure of different forms of mobile computers, and subsequently affected their physical design in the wider marketplace. Yet despite an ever-increasing range of related products including tablet and handheld computers, the most successful form of all remains the laptop computer. The laptop has proved to be a remarkably durable and popular machine. Its flexibility as a product coupled with its portability, functionality and semantic associations have made the laptop the general-purpose computer product of choice. The now ubiquitous nature of mobile computing means that the market for laptops has diversified greatly since the product type's introduction. Lower-priced laptops are now marketed by department stores purely

as commodity items, and lower-spec laptops are routinely given away 'free' when purchased with a broadband contract. The competition for providing laptops at the lowest possible price is fierce. At the other end of this scale of commodification, more advanced and expensive versions of laptops remain objects of desire. In 2007 Sony published a series of full-page adverts for their upmarket Vaio range of laptops, which appeared in full colour in a number of glossy magazines and national newspaper weekend supplements. The images, bearing the strapline 'be like no other', clearly delineated the Sony products from their more mainstream competitors and, denying the

Brochure for the GRiD 'Briefcase Computer', 1985.

products' existence as the result of the mass production process, suggested that to own these particular laptops would transfer to the owner a level of individuality and status reserved only for those owners of high-end luxury items. This has similarities to the associative use of aeroplanes and helicopters in manufacturers' brochures a quarter of a century earlier, but on a much more accessible, more easily attainable scale. It is more in line with those companies that appropriate widely recognized celebrities to endorse their products in adverts, suggesting that to own one of their company's (for example) wristwatches will at least associate the owner with (if not transfer the lifestyle of) a famous actor or sportsperson.

The images of the Sony laptops were associated not with a well-known personality, but with unidentified models. The models, though, were clearly exactly that – they were not taking the role of a 'typical

Sony Vaio Laptop adverts, 2007. The laptop as fashion accessory for both sexes.

user' in order to contextualize the object in its intended environment or explain the use of the product to an unfamiliar audience. This was fashion photography, and the models displayed a carefully selected wardrobe of clothes and accessories. Despite being the central focus of the advert, the laptops here acted as markers of brand affiliation – fashion accessories, yet accessories of such standing that their value was not in question. Their value was in fact amplified by this context. The unique quality transferred to the potential owner of the Sony laptop was to be more than acceptably stylish. Upward mobility made tangible. This is technology as fashion, technology as identity, individuality and self-image. Computers on the catwalk. There was also an element of regendering the laptop in these adverts. Many of the more elite models of laptops became available in a number of different colourways or patterns in a similar fashion to mobile phones, as manufacturers strove to attract the attention of a much younger and more discriminating audience. Surely it was no mistake that the male model had a blue computer and the female a pink one? Certainly the different adverts appeared in magazines aimed at the relevant gender.

As well as being a fashionable item to be seen with, and in spite of its long history and now ubiquity, certain laptops still manage to retain a cachet of cool. 'Executive' business versions are still advertised that certainly have a level of kudos above that of their desktop counterparts. The man in the Panasonic Toughbook advert of 2008 may be more Jason Bourne than James Bond, but the fact remains that although there is a perfectly justified market for rugged portable computers, for field workers from building sites to oil rigs, the average executive needs their capabilities as much as they need an off-road 4 × 4 with bull bars to drive around city centres. In this context, the macho image of the rugged portable computer is all. It seems that even if it is no longer quite the status symbol it once

Panasonic 'Toughbook Executive' advert, 2008. For some, the laptop remains a signifier of excitement, freedom and adventure.

was, at least to some, the laptop remains a signifier of excitement, freedom and adventure.

Across the course of its history, then, be it in the form of the office computer, the home computer or the mobile computer, computers have had an element of political power as a direct result of the socio-political landscapes in which they operated. These landscapes have, of course, changed dramatically since the computer first became a part of people's lives, and as a result, computers now have less agency than they did. This is largely because they have become so commonplace that computers now slip below our cognitive radars. In the workplace, computers are so familiar that they are now only noticeable by their absence. Managers have even been known to remove their computer to be operated by a secretary and reclaim the valuable real estate of the surface of their desks in order to display managerial authority. In the home, the computer is not a luxury but a very real necessity for many. Their extensive use by children and teenagers for education and internet access, in particular for social networking activities,[49] is such that those without them consider themselves to be at a distinct social disadvantage. The sheer ubiquity of mobile computing, be it in the form of laptops, PDAs, Blackberrys or smartphones has, for the most part, made it a completely quotidian activity. Although, as can be seen from the furore with which the latest models are advertised and the enthusiasm with which they are sought out,[50] such products retain a high level of desirability and are often displayed with pride. Computers may no longer have the same status or gender associations they once had, but they still play a significant role in defining who we are.

4 | Futuristic Fantasies

When in 1833 Charles Babbage demonstrated a prototype of his Difference Engine to an amazed audience, 'visitors gazed at the working of the beautiful instrument with a sort of expression, and dare I say the same sort of feeling, that some savages are said to have shown on first seeing a looking glass or hearing a gun'.[1]

As a completely new and unfamiliar object, the reactions of Babbage's audience to his Difference Engine are quite understandable. A machine that could add and subtract, multiply and divide? Otherworldly magic? A piece of parlour trickery? Babbage's Difference Engine promised not only to calculate mathematical differences, but also to really make a difference – to change the world. Calculating machines eventually developed into huge electro-mechanical marvels, yet by the time the electronic computer appeared over a century later, public reactions to such technology remained remarkably similar. The particular forms and fora in which electronic computers were first presented, and the recorded reactions to them, reveal a great deal. Computers were clearly seen as impressive and inspirational, fearsome and frightening in equal terms. The different ways in which computing technology was represented in popular culture reveals more about how such objects were perceived and the particular hopes and fears they effected. Furthermore, this representation directly affected the relationship between people and computers – as representation reflects and amplifies, so it informs and reinforces existing attitudes.

The rapid development of the electronic computer from a scientific curiosity into a widely recognized and understood object coincided perfectly with an age of unprecedented public interest in science and technology. Following the destructive potential of technology witnessed during two world wars, world fairs and festivals celebrated the potential of technological breakthroughs and scientific discoveries to create a brighter future for all concerned. The launch of the Russian satellite Sputnik-1 in 1957 marked the dawn of the space age, and when Russia followed this achievement in 1961 by making Yuri Gagarin the first man to be put into space, the 'space race' became a defining characteristic of the relationship between the USA and the Soviet Union. The aim to be the first to reach the moon was a powerful nationalistic and political driving force, leading to such hyperbole as 'We can beat the Reds with this plan for shooting our flag to the Moon by rocket.'[2] The possibility of putting a man on the Moon made space travel, with its associated acceptance of advanced technology, a part of the spirit of the age. But the perceived potential of the computer to recreate the world as a better place was soon tempered by the realization of the huge costs and sacrifices such change would incur, and by the potential for technology to destroy far more than it would ever create. As part of this milieu, the computer, presented as an artificial intelligence, was a futuristic fantasy made real, and its relationship to science fiction was an obvious although not totally accurate connection to make. Fascination with technology ran through all of popular culture and affected the ways in which images and objects appeared, and, it might be assumed, none more so than the computer. But what was the connection between the presentation of computing and the reality? Was there a relationship between the physical design of real computers and their representation in science fiction? In fact, the connection was very much a two-way street.

Front-Page News

One of the war's top secrets, an amazing machine which applies electronic speeds for the first time to mathematical tasks hitherto too difficult and cumbersome for solution, was announced here tonight.[3]

In stark contrast to the secrecy surrounding the development of the 'Colossus' at Bletchley Park, the story of ENIAC was front-page news. The *New York Times* heralded the birth of the electronic computer on 15 February 1946. At the evening presentation in Philadelphia, ENIAC successfully ran a ballistics trajectory that had been programmed by six female staff and in doing so 'captured the world's imagination'.[4] The publicity was widespread, and the United States War Department even held the first computer conference to explain how the ENIAC worked.

Talk about open source! Every major corporation and university sent representatives . . . And there you have it. The computer was born at Bletchley Park but the computer industry was born in the good old U.S. of A.[5]

Interest in the potential of this new technology ran high, and stories about the latest innovations appeared regularly in newspapers. National pride was at stake, and in response to the US success of the ENIAC, the press in the UK quickly reported on the ongoing work on the Pilot ACE at the National Physical Laboratory. A 1946 report titled 'Britain to Make a Radio Brain' told how the '"ACE" would be superior to the US model' with a bigger memory, and was so advanced that it would take three years to build.[6] By 1950, the same news-paper reported that a part of this 'British Robot' was on display at the Royal Society,[7] but computer technology was already moving faster than expected. By that time, the ACE was old news. The world's attention had been diverted to the achievement of Manchester University and their development of the first stored program computer in 1948. A BBC news item reported that the complex mathematical problems of calculating enormous prime numbers could be solved by this '"electronic brain" in 25 minutes instead of by a human brain in six months'[8] (although admittedly, setting the machine up to solve such a problem took a week). The achievement was also reported in *The Illustrated London News* in June 1949, with a special panoramic image of the Manchester Mark 1 machine made up from 24 separate photographs.[9] Less than two years later, Ferranti developed a commercial version of the same computer, the Ferranti Mk 1, and in 1951 the BBC recorded a special edition of the popular radio programme *Children's Hour*[10] in which listeners heard the machine perform pieces of music – 'Baa Baa Black Sheep', 'God Save the King', and 'In the Mood' (which remain the earliest existing recordings of computer-generated music).[11]

The marvellous new invention remained at the centre of public attention, with stories regularly appearing about each new possible application for the computer. In the US, the creators of the ENIAC received wide publicity in 1951 through the role played by their first commercial product, the UNIVAC, in compiling and analysing the contents of the US Census.[12] In fact, over the following decade, the activities of UNIVAC were consistently considered newsworthy, with articles appearing covering everything from its part in locating the 'lost' eighth moon of Jupiter,[13] to its use in specifying the most suitable shade of lipstick for women![14] However, the UNIVAC was never more in the headlines or made more of an impact on the public

consciousness than when it correctly predicted the outcome of the US presidential election in 1952. Unsure as how to refer to the computer or how to portray it to the public in their article about the election, the *New York Times* referred to UNIVAC as both a 'Brain' and 'an electronic robot eight feet tall'.[15] The public had the chance to make their own minds up about the computer when they saw the machine in action during the televised event hosted by Walter Cronkite. The opinion polls had all indicated that the Democrat candidate Adlai Stevenson was the front-runner for election, but based on the results of the very first returns, UNIVAC predicted an unexpected landslide success for Dwight D. Eisenhower. This was considered to be so wide of the mark that the CBS television network prevented the prediction from being broadcast live and only admitted the cover-up when the computer forecast turned out to

In a live television broadcast, Walter Cronkite and J. Presper Eckert (the computer's co-inventor) used the UNIVAC to correctly predict the outcome of the 1952 US Presidential election.

have been absolutely right! The uncanny accuracy of the computer had been widely witnessed and 'helped further solidify the hopes and fears that the general public had about these wondrous but scary machines'.[16] Following this celebrated event, it became standard practice to include computer predictions in important election proceedings.

Similarly in the UK, the media continued to pay attention to the latest technology. One of the earliest public presentations of an electronic computer was at the Exhibition of Science in South Kensington in 1951, as part of the Festival of Britain. Here, in a purpose-built extension to the Science Museum, a special version of the Ferranti Mk 1 made a powerful impression.

Like everyone else, I came to a standstill before the electric brain, or, as they prefer to call it, the 'Nimrod Digital Computer'. This looks like a

Visitors to the Festival of Britain in 1951 play 'Nim' against a version of the Ferranti Mark I called 'Nimrod'.

tremendous grey refrigerator and it has more wiring in it than the rest of the exhibition put together. And I'm not surprised – it's absolutely terrifying. What you do, if you have the courage, is to volunteer to play a game against this machine.[17]

The game Nimrod was designed to play was 'Nim' – a game traditionally played with multiple groups of counters or matchsticks. The use of a game to demonstrate the capabilities of a computer was a deliberate (and established) move to present the machine as 'friendly' technology,[18] but the manufacturers took pains to ensure it was not seen as frivolous:

It may appear that, in trying to make machines play games, we are wasting our time. This is not true as the theory of games is extremely complex and a machine that can play a complex game can also be programmed to carry out very complex practical problems. It is interesting to note for example that the computation necessary to play Nim is very similar to that required to examine the economies of a country in which neither a state of monopoly nor of free trade exists.[19]

In the game of Nim, two players take it in turns to remove a number of matches at a time. The winner is the player left with a single match at the end of the game. Nimrod had a front panel covered in a series of lights to display the moves of the game, and to show the particular internal registers being used to calculate the next move. This gave the observers of the machine a visual indication of the processes being carried out within the computer, and gave the computer the appearance, at least, of some kind of 'machine intelligence' at work. The manufacturers were keen to dispel the notion that computers had such worrying faculty, writing in the accompanying booklet that they were opposed to the common use of the term 'electronic brain' as the 'use of the word "brain" can lead to great confusion'.[20] But these reassurances often fell on deaf ears. The observer who found the machine so terrifying supposed that 'at the next exhibition they'll have real heaps of matches and awful steel arms will come out of the machine to pick them up!'[21] The view of the computer as a mechanical being was understandable. Computers were inevitably seen as machines that could think, their pulsing lights betraying a monstrous sentience, although of course, the use of lights was never intended to be anything other than purely functional. The association of indicator lights with computing processes is thought to have originated with the ENIAC, as the team behind it searched for a way to impress those who could authorize funding for its further development. According to some reports, ping-pong balls were cut in half and placed over lamps that would provide an illuminated 'trajectory' of ballistics, while others suggest that numbers were painted onto light bulbs, which were then screwed into the ENIAC's panels to show the machine at work. The consensus is, though, that 'dynamic, flashy lights would thereafter be associated with the computer in the public mind.'[22] One author states that this publicity stunt 'provided an enduring trope for machine intelligence that remains with us today. In both science fiction movies and contemporary product design, small, light-emitting diodes have become almost mandatory features that often have no other function other than to mark the willingness of a machine to cooperate with human efforts to make it work.'[23]

The British public were soon presented with another 'benevolent' computer in 1957 with the live radio and television broadcast of the first draw of Premium Bonds by the computer ERNIE (Electronic Random Number Indicator Equipment). ERNIE, based in Lytham St Annes near Blackpool, was a special-purpose, non-programmable computer housed in a series of tall, rectangular steel cabinets, controlled from

a large hand-built, double pedestal steel console. The console was equipped with two telephones and an angled control panel mounted with switches, buttons, lights and a large clock. Nobody knew about the previous activities of the team that built ERNIE at the Post Office Research Station at Dollis Hill in London, but it was in fact the same team who had developed the 'Colossus' computer for the Government Code and Cipher School at Bletchley Park. In a single move, they had gone from creating the world's most secret computer to creating one of the most widely publicized. ERNIE was a hybrid machine containing both vacuum tubes and transistors, and it generated random digits by creating noise through gas discharge neon diodes in a bank of vacuum tubes. The presentation of ERNIE as the public's friend was extensive and long lasting. Throughout the 1950s and '60s, 'winning

ERNIE, 1957. Built by the same team that developed the Colossus at Bletchley Park, Postmaster General Ernest Marples turns on ERNIE and starts the first draw for Premium Bonds.

numbers were announced by celebrities of the day, including Bruce Forsyth, Norman Wisdom and Bob Hope'.[24]

Through all this exposure – newspaper coverage, radio broadcasts and television appearances – the computer began to move from being a laboratory-based rarity to a fixture of people's everyday lives. From ENIAC to ERNIE, the public were presented with computers as complex, large-scale machines – machines which were powerful yet essentially benign. Computers calculated equations, solved problems, played games, predicted election results and selected lucky winners at random. They were not presented in any way as a threat, yet it was not long before their potential to change the established order was realized. The popularity of a machine such as ERNIE was not a standard reaction to the onslaught of new technology; responses were understandably mixed. The technological revolution intimated by the appearance of the computer was a case of history repeating itself. As with the mechanization of manual labour processes during the Industrial Revolution, the mechanization of mental processes enabled by the computer promised great progress and yet was also a portent of job losses and social upheaval. Consequently, by the mid-1950s, the new spectacle of the 'electronic brain' was a subject of great concern to many, and was discussed widely in the media, forming the cover stories of international news magazines where their huge size and potential were colourfully described. A 1955 article in *Time* magazine called 'The Brain Builders' was a typical example:

> This quintessential brain looked like nothing more than a collection of filing cases, stretching in a 60-ft. semicircle about the room. From within the grey metal cases came a faint humming sound; along the light-studded metallic face were scores of twinkling orange sparks, rippling like waves of thought . . . Along one end of the chamber was a gleaming

plate-glass observation window, through which mere humans – attendants and sightseers – could watch and marvel.

The brain was the newest electronic calculator, developed by International Business Machines Corp. and installed in Monsanto Chemical Co.'s St. Louis headquarters. To IBM, it was the 'Model 702 Electronic Data Processing Machine'. To Monsanto and awed visitors, it was simply 'the giant brain'. Seated at its control console, a man has at his command the computing ability of 25,000 trained mathematicians.[25]

'The computing ability of 25,000 trained mathematicians.' It is no surprise people were worried. The view of computers as electronic brains that could perform so much better than human beings was a frightening one, and as public awareness of computers grew, the perception of them moved from being benevolent curiosities to a potential menace. Their ability to outperform their human counterparts presented a clear threat to people's livelihoods, and their introduction had to be dealt with sensitively. In order to 'reduce possible resistance to the new computers', the house magazine of the insurance company Metropolitan Life reassured workers that ordering two new UNIVACs would not entail any reduction of clerical staff.[26] Yet employers often got carried away with the prospective economic payback. When companies such as General Electric tried to justify the purchase of a UNIVAC, the benefits were 'almost entirely cast in terms of its ability to replace salaried clerks and their overhead costs',[27] and the promotional essay explaining their intentions to their workers ended with a quotation describing 'the Utopia of automatic production'! Despite all the reassurances, the spreading adoption of computers raised significant concerns among workers, and these worries were often reflected in the ways computers were represented in popular culture. An early representation of this fear, just a few years after the launch of commercial electronic computers, occurred in the 1957

Hollywood film *Desk Set* starring Katharine Hepburn and Spencer Tracy. *Desk Set* revolved around the introduction of a fictional 'electronic brain' named EMERAC into the research department of a broadcasting company. EMERAC bore an uncanny resemblance to the UNIVAC, with the addition of a huge backboard of illuminated lights with which the computer could communicate messages to its operators. The computer's ability to retrieve facts and figures at lightning speed is taken by the researchers in the department as making their roles redundant, which leads to a pitched battle between the workers and the computer experts. Eventually, after a number of computer-generated mishaps that nearly bring the company to its knees, the limitations of the machine become reassuringly apparent.

Mechanical Men

EMERAC in *Desk Set* was far closer to reality than many other early representations of computers. At least EMERAC was a static machine – there are many more examples of computers at this point represented as mechanical men. The computer, like many new and unfamiliar

Shortly after the UNIVAC appeared in American offices, EMERAC appeared in the 1957 film *Desk Set*, reflecting people's fears that computers would take over their jobs.

creations before it, was the subject of a certain level of technopho-bia, and as such became the target of cartoonists in the popular press. Cartoonists often anthropomorphized computers as huge static beings with human features, often depicted with steam or smoke billowing out of them as they struggled with difficult questions: an attempt, perhaps, to reassure people that we humans were still superior and that computers couldn't always provide the answers. Another notable feature of these caricatures was the intimation of an artificial intel-ligence – they could read written instructions and provide answers written on pieces of paper, which somewhat betrayed people's lack of understanding about the realities of computing. Occasionally, these cartoons were recognizable as actual people – because of their con-nection with the establishment, usually leading politicians of the day. Harold Wilson's famous speech at the Labour Party Annual Confer-ence in Scarborough in 1963, in which he discussed 'the Britain that

Cartoon from the *Daily Mail*, 1959.

Cummings

THE GREAT WILSON
WONDER COMPUTER
KNOWS ALL THE ANSWERS
as advertised on T.V. before the Election

"At least my Minister of Technology might have shown me how to mend a fuse"

is going to be forged in the white heat of this [scientific and technological] revolution', associated Wilson and the Labour government with technological progress for the duration of his leadership.

Computers at this point were something of an unknown quantity, and the lack of understanding of what they actually were only added to people's wariness of them. This confusion was reflected in the way that the terms 'computer' and 'robot' were used so interchangeably, and led to the view that as mechanical beings, they could do anything that people could do. As a 1958 article put it:

The age of science has made the word 'robot' the focus of popular fears and hopes. The hope is that machines with minds, machines that can talk, think, and work like men, will give everyone a life of leisure. The fear is that robots will replace mankind, that they might run amuck and

Cartoon from the *Daily Express*, 1965. Confusing 'electronic brains' and 'robots', early computers were often depicted as mechanical men.

destroy their masters, that the robots will get us if we don't watch out. What was conceived as a work-saving machine has become the popular bogeyman of the age of science.[28]

Numerous articles speculated on the impact of computing on society, and came to different conclusions. There are numerous examples of writings that celebrated the arrival of the computer as well as ones that took a much darker view. The more positive articles often voiced the opinion that if a computer could do so much work, then they could make life easier for everyone in the future. Such a piece appeared in the 1953 article 'The ROBOTS Are Coming!' which stated: 'Our civilization is being invaded by a horde of mechanical men who are determined to change our way of life. But there's no need to worry. It's all in the spirit of good fellowship.' The article described a typical day in the life of an American citizen in a few years time, when automatic machines and computers take the strain out of every aspect of existence, from breakfast being automatically prepared to going to work in a car which drives itself. Quite what people would do – other than watch – when machines do everything is not really discussed. In a slightly more serious article from 1955 titled 'How Automation Will Affect Your Job', the message was 'new skills, a shorter work week and more leisure time will be yours in 1975 – thanks to machines with "brains"!'[29] The article imagined the workplace in 20 years time, and was more realistic about the fact that significant job losses would occur; but for those remaining in work, a four-day week was expected. Increased leisure time would lead to an increase in service industries and lifelong education opportunities, all paid for by the increased manufacturing output enabled by computers and automation. This view of reduced workloads was widely held and was reflected in numerous fictional future settings. The imagined lifestyle was perfectly parodied by Hanna-Barbera

Productions in their 1962 space-age cartoon, *The Jetsons*. The family's father, George Jetson, worked three hours a day, three days a week, at a job that consisted purely of pushing a single button, while at home, his wife watched a robot do all the housework! In fact, anxiety around what society would do with such increased leisure time continued for many years, and even in the 1970s, UK television programmes such as *Tomorrow's World* held debates about the issue, while union leaders predicted the imminent arrival of the 24-hour working week.[30] If only.

The more negative image of the computer as a malevolent 'bogeyman' is closely linked to the representation of the computer as a robot. When the flashing lights of early computers were joined by tape storage units, there was an even stronger impression that the machine was 'thinking' as it trawled backwards and forwards through the ribbon of its memory to find certain facts. There was a tendency for illustrators to turn the computer into a robot with mechanical limbs, and those same moving tape reels were obvious candidates to give the inanimate machine a pair of eyes. Now, the computer could be even more easily anthropomorphized into a mechanical man – a development of the very same mechanical man that had dominated science fiction before computers existed. This type of anthropomorphism accentuated the link between the computer and its ability to do human work, and perhaps reinforced the message that computers would soon be doing all type of jobs – and not just physically demanding ones, but ones requiring significant mental skills. These were not just labour-saving devices, but potentially artificial intelligences – the very stuff of science fiction.

In terms of the representation of computers in popular culture, it is often assumed that computers must have featured widely in science fiction long before they became real manufactured objects. Actually, this is untrue: the vast majority of science fiction writing

never envisaged a static machine as the technological saviour or nemesis of mankind – that role was imagined for the robot. Prior to its appearance in reality, 'the SF genre paid almost no attention to the computer'.[31] However, as usual, there are some curious exceptions that prove the rule. In a 1945 serialized novel in *Astounding Science Fiction*, A. E. van Vogt published 'World of Ā', in which he described a large, complex machine entity, which through 'subsidiary brains' could administer thousands of tasks simultaneously, although the mechanics of his 'games machine' were not detailed. It was not just the text that was remarkably forward-looking, as an illustration accompanying the story showed a character using a video communicator which looks remarkably like a flat-screen monitor![32] Another forward-looking piece, 'A Logic Named Joe', was a humorous short story written by Murray Leinster, which described the unintended

The Jetsons, 1962. The future of work: three hours a day, three days a week, George Jetson pushes a single button.

consequences of using a series of small machines called 'logics', similar in many ways to networked home computers – and that was published in the same year ENIAC was announced, in 1946! The machines in these stories clearly had strong similarities to the capabilities of computers but did not use the actual term, but then at that time real computers were also regularly referred to by other names. It could also be argued that as the description of the technology used in them was so circumspect, they could be seen as extrapolations of the precursor to the electronic computer – the mechanical calculator. For the most part, however, science fiction focused on anthropomorphizing machinery into a variety of vaguely humanoid figures as an obvious form in which technology could either serve, or alternatively threaten, civilization. Technology was often regarded as a help to mankind, and the connection between human and mechanical servants was an easy link to make. Images of 'mechanical men' that could act as robotic butlers had been a common theme in cartoons as far back as the early 1900s, as people looked forward to the exciting possibilities of the twentieth century. The familiarity of

Illustration for the story 'World of Ā', 1945.

ARE THEY
FOR US OR AGAINST US?

robots as an element of science fiction in the mind of the public perhaps explains the easy interchangeability of the terms 'robot' and
'computer' at that point. Robots had appeared regularly on the covers
of pulp magazines such as *Amazing Stories* and *Astounding Stories*
since the 1920s, and memorable robotic characters such as 'Maria'
in Fritz Lang's 1929 film *Metropolis* through to 'Robby' in the 1956
film *Forbidden Planet* had brought the concept of the robot into the
mainstream and made it a well-understood symbol of man's future
triumphs and tribulations with technology. When placed alongside
the anthropomorphic representations of early computers as 'electronic brains' and 'mechanical men', the images of the two devices were
very similar and therefore easily confused, which likely led to the assumption that computers had long been an object of science fantasy.

Once computers and their potential impact were part of the public's awareness of technology, they became central to many films.

RCA advert, 1970. The depiction of computers as monsters was so widespread, that even
manufacturers used the image to discuss their positive and negative points.

Apart from the more immediate and very real threat to employment as portrayed in *Desk Set*, many films, particularly science fiction films, looked further forward and reflected fears about man's ability to fully control advanced technology. Perhaps one of the most famous examples of such loss of control in the science fiction genre is HAL – the artificial intelligence controlling the spaceship *Discovery One* in Stanley Kubrick's and Arthur C. Clarke's 1968 film *2001: A Space Odyssey*. The human crew of the spaceship is almost helpless when the malfunctioning HAL 9000 computer decides to kill them because they intend to disconnect it. In many ways, the portrayal of HAL is an example of technological extrapolation that missed a social innovation. At the time Kubrick and Clarke worked on the screenplay for the film, computers were large, room-sized mainframes. HAL, even though massively more powerful than computers of the day, takes the same form of an individual, large machine – large enough for the ship's captain to enter and disable the computer when it malfunctions. Kubrick, and certainly the scientist Clarke, would have been well aware of the electronic engineer Gordon

Still from *2001: A Space Odyssey*, 1968. The future computer was still seen as big enough to walk inside.

Moore's widely promoted prediction of the exponential increase of computing power (known later as 'Moore's Law'), which was first published in 1965.[33] This originally predicted that the power of a computer would double every year for the next ten years (he later changed this to a doubling every two years, which has held true now for over 40 years). Extrapolating forward and applying this theory to the powerful capabilities of the computer 33 years in the future, therefore, was in some respects straightforward, including the advent of artificial intelligence and voice control (which are a reality, although not nearly as successful as predicted). However, predicting the future designed form of the computer is another matter entirely. The expected model of computer usage, of centralized computers accessed by numerous people, eventually proved not to meet the needs of users. Additionally, as Engelbart had noted, the corollary of increasing the number of transistors on a single silicon chip (as in Moore's Law) is the reduction in size of the transistor, allowing smaller (as well as more powerful) computers to be built.[34] It might seem strange that such an informed futurologist as Arthur C. Clarke would get the future of computing so wrong, and might lead one to wonder if the size of HAL was a deliberate choice intended to imbue the omniscient, all-seeing computer with an air of malevolence that

Still from *Billion Dollar Brain*, 1967.

could never emanate from, say, a handheld device. Although, if it was accidental, such a mistake would not have been unusual, as even those people closely involved in the computer industry did not foresee the transformation of computing technology usage from a small number of large machines to an enormous number of individual, personal computers. A number of well-known and often quoted predictions from the industry point to this fact[35] – almost unbelievably, the Chairman of IBM, Thomas Watson, when discussing electro-mechanical machines said in 1943: 'I think there is a world market for maybe five computers'! In 1949 the magazine *Popular Mechanics* predicted that 'computers in the future may weigh no more than 1.5 tons', and as recently as 1977, Kenneth Olsen, of Digital Equipment Corporation (DEC), said that 'there is no reason anyone would want a computer in the home', despite this being the year that three very popular home computers were launched! Such outdated soundbites sound comical, but it has to be remembered that they were grounded in the ways that computers used to be used rather than how they turned out to be used.

The loss of control over computers around a more immediately pressing issue was tied up with mounting fears around nuclear warfare. The increasing role of technology in the defence of the nation had been widely promoted in the US, with, for example, the introduction in 1956 of the SAGE Air Defense System being described in detail in Cold War propaganda films such as *On Guard!* and *In Your Defense*.[36] Political developments such as the 1962 Cuban Missile Crisis and the public realization that more, and more crucial aspects of the nation's defences were becoming reliant on impersonal computer systems raised a number of concerns over the reliability and security of such arrangements. There was some apprehension around our ability to retain control over computers, and the significant potential for an 'accidental' apocalypse or the deliberate misuse of such vast power. Films that reflected these particular concerns located huge computerized systems in remote underground command bunkers and cast them and their use as central to the plot. Ken Russell's 1967 film *Billion Dollar Brain*, based on a novel by Len Deighton, depicted the secret agent Harry Palmer thwarting a plan by a billionaire oil baron to use a supercomputer to initiate a third World War for his own economic ends. The 'brain' itself was portrayed as a series of large computer consoles and multiple tape storage units, much like those of the SAGE system, with the advanced power of the computer made more threatening through the sheer magnitude of the installation. *Colossus: The Forbin Project*, made in 1970 (before the creation of the real 'Colossus' at Bletchley Park became public knowledge) was based on a 1966 novel which predicted separate artificially intelligent supercomputers set up to oversee the nuclear defences of the USA and the USSR joining forces, and ultimately using man's own nuclear weapons to control society for its own good.

In a similar vein, in the 1983 children's science fiction film *War-Games*, a schoolchild accidentally hacks into the National Defence supercomputer WOPR (War Operation Plan Response, pronounced 'whopper') using an IMSAI 8080 home computer over a telephone link. Believing it to be the system of a computer games company, the child engages the machine in a simulated war game, almost resulting in Armageddon. Visually, WOPR is depicted as a bulky, battleship-grey, inscrutable steel cabinet with largely rounded corners and the obligatory flashing lights; housed in its own air-conditioned room and operated by specialist attendants. In many ways, WOPR is presented as an updated version of an early mainframe computer – styled very similarly to machines such as the Ferranti Pegasus of 1956. The deliberate 'retro-styling' of WOPR is interesting to note, recalling as it does the 'behemoth' nature of the early mainframe and its associated air of unpredictability.

Still from *Colossus: The Forbin Project*, 1970. Numerous films reflected the fear of computer-controlled defence systems going out of control.

Still from *WarGames*, 1983.

After the paranoia of the Cold War faded, attention turned more to other ways in which society's increasing reliance on computers might backfire. For example, the susceptibility of financial computer systems to infiltration and the potentially dire economic consequences of unauthorized use became an ongoing concern, one which was addressed in numerous films including *Hackers* (1995), *Firewall* (2006) and *Diehard 4.0* (2007). Reflecting the increasingly ubiquitous nature of computing, the physical representation of the computers themselves ceased to be central to the plots of these films, and computing appeared instead as 'naturalized' technology. The advanced nature of the computers being used was often implied instead by the use of alternative and seemingly radical methods of interacting with them. Intended to be glimpses into the far future of Human–Computer Interaction technology, in reality, these interfaces were not quite as futuristic as they were made out to be. In fact they were more often than not merely extrapolations of existing, fledgling technology demonstrated by research laboratories at universities or software corporations. One of the most common, appearing in a diverse range of books, programmes and films from *2001: A Space Odyssey* and *Star Trek* to comedy series such as *The Hitchhiker's Guide to the Galaxy* and *Red Dwarf* is speech recognition, the ability to command a computer purely by speaking directly to it. This has long been the Holy Grail of Human-Computer Interaction and Artificial Intelligence research, going at least as far back as the mid-1960s to doctoral research at Stanford University[37] and its development into the 'Hearsay' speech understanding system in the computer science department at Carnegie Mellon University in the early 1970s. The assumption that such systems would be easily perfected and make all other methods of interaction obsolete is highlighted in the 1986 film *Star Trek IV: The Voyage Home*, when the crew of the *Enterprise* travel back in time to Earth: engineer 'Scotty' is given a computer mouse (which had appeared on the market only a few years earlier) to control a computer, and proceeds to use it as a microphone.

The use of virtual reality environments as computer interfaces made appearances in a number of films in the 1990s, including *Lawn-mower Man* (1992), *Disclosure* (1994) and *Johnny Mnemonic* (1995), although the technology these futuristic systems were based on was first demonstrated a quarter of a century earlier in 1968 by Ivan Sutherland (the inventor of the 'Sketchpad' computer graphics system), while he was an Associate Professor at Harvard University. *Disclosure*, based on a Michael Crichton novel of the same year, demonstrated a ludicrously complicated walkthrough experience inside a comput-erized three-dimensional filing system, which involved the user wear-ing a headset containing small monitors and standing on a rolling pad to walk through a digitally created virtual temple lined with virtual filing cabinets of electronic documents. A guide to help users navigate this temple appeared in the form of a digitally generated 'angel', and users could interact with each other's wireframe avatars while 'inside' the system. Ridiculously overblown as a method of merely storing and retrieving electronic documents, the representa-tion of such an interface serves only to highlight an infatuation with technological excess.

Much more practical, perhaps, was the kind of computer interface portrayed in the film *Tron* in 1982, in which the whole surface of a large executive desk was shown to be one giant touch-sensitive com-puter screen. This seemed a long way from the available keyboard operated, text-based interfaces of the day, but actually was not that far removed from reality. Research had already started into touch displays in the late 1960s and was being conducted in a number of places, with prototype transparent touchscreens first appearing at the end of the 1970s. Prototype graphical interfaces had been developed at Xerox, and commercial versions were just around the corner at

the time of the film's release. Much work has been done in this area since, with the development of 'multi-touch' interfaces such as those on the Apple iPhone, which interpret different strokes made on screen with more than one finger. Even more advanced systems have been developed by Apple, Microsoft and Linux, which form the basis of 'surface computing', an interface format in which large, electronic desktop surfaces interact with other devices such as mobile phones or digital cameras placed on them. Such systems allow the easy manipulation of electronic documents. Simply touching documents and sliding them around by hand, for example, allows the transfer of files between different devices. Quite how people will take to a computer

Still from *Star Trek IV: The Voyage Home*, 1986. *Star Trek* popularized the view that future computers would be voice controlled.

Still from *Disclosure*, 1994. A pixellated avatar of Michael Douglas explores a virtual filing system.

moving away from being a small or portable item back to being an immovable large-scale object like a table or desk is questionable, but the 'natural' feel of moving large items across a desktop as if they were real documents certainly has its appeal. A 'logical' development of these touch-based systems was shown in the film *Minority Report* in 2002, in the form of a large-scale, non-touch 'gesture recognition' interface. In the film, the operator stands in front of a large, vertical transparent glass screen displaying a series of files and documents and, using a pair of special gloves, manipulates the files by the waving of arms and hands, conducting an orchestra of information. Again based on the latest real technological developments rather than a writer's imagination, the director of the film, Steven Spielberg, had consulted with Microsoft during the making of the film to discuss their research into gesture recognition technology. Systems have been developed in which cameras not only track the movements of an operator's limbs, but also recognize the items they are holding and reproduce images of them on screen. Technically feasible though they may be, such vertical interfaces have been proved to be extremely uncomfortable for anything but the shortest periods of use, but obviously, they look incredibly impressive.

Still from *Tron*, 1982.

This concentration on methods of interaction rather than on the computers themselves, reveals a high level of acceptance of computing technology. Any fear of computers as objects seems to have disappeared at this point, but was replaced instead by a fear of the intangible phenomenon of the internet. The possibilities and dangers inherent in wide access to and misuse of personal information are reflected in films such as *The Net* (1995) and *Enemy of the State* (1998), which are examples of a genre that shows the debilitating effects of computer experts being able to remove all traces of a person's identity from computer databases and the ability to monitor their every move through computer-controlled surveillance. Where the misuse of computing technology remains a cause of concern, the form of the computer itself, as a naturalized product, no longer reflects our hopes or fears.

As shown, since electronic computers first appeared, they have been presented by manufacturers and represented in the media in a variety of ways, and these presentations and representations have predictably reflected our opinions of them. Because of the power and pervasiveness of popular culture, an interesting question that follows from this observation is to what extent, if any, have these

Still from *Minority Report*, 2002. No keyboard required: future computers operated by sweeping gestures.

presentations and representations had any agency in the consequent design of computers themselves?

Computers have always been presented as powerful and progressive pieces of technology. Suggestions of their potential power and speed can be seen in the names given to some of the earliest machines. The contrived and largely meaningless acronyms given to many research-based computers such as ENIAC, BINAC, UNIVAC and EDSAC meant little to anyone, and computers soon began to bear far more evocative titles. The British computer manufacturing company Ferranti, for example, named their machines after various mythological characters. The 1951 'Nimrod' was named after the biblical ruler of Mesopotamia, and the 1956 'Pegasus' after the Greek winged horse of Poseidon. 'Mercury', a solid-state version of the Manchester Mk 1, was developed in 1957 and named after the Roman messenger and god of commerce (or of course, the planet). 'Argus', (the son of Zeus) was the name given to an industrial control computer Ferranti developed for the Military in 1958, and 'Orion' (the Greek hunter, or the constellation) was the name given to their 1959 mainframe computer. The mythological names continued with a joint project between the University of Manchester, Ferranti and Plessey that produced the early supercomputer 'Atlas' of 1962, which in turn led to the 'Titan', developed by Ferranti and the University of Cambridge. J. Lyons & Co. produced the first commercially designed computer specifically for business use and gave it the acronym 'LEO' (Lyons Electronic Office), connoting a powerful (and very British) symbol as well as an astrological sign. Through such names, computers were presented as fantastical objects – potent forces to be reckoned with.

The early association of computers with mythological beings, and through them the stars and planets after which they were named, quickly linked computers with outer space. This association was compounded when, in the huge burst of activity in the computer industry

in the mid-1970s, a whole range of companies with science-fiction-sounding names became associated with the manufacture of computers. Raytheon, meaning 'light of the gods', was a company that had been producing electrical components since the 1920s, and worked with MIT on their wartime radar research before producing computer components and systems in the 1970s. Tektronix produced electronic components from 1946 and moved into computer terminals and microcomputers in the 1970s, as did Xerox, who took their name from xerography, meaning 'dry writing' in Greek, in 1961. No trace remains of other 1980s companies such as Xenotron, which produced CAD workstations or Nexos, which produced desk-sized word processors. Even companies without such futuristic sounding names often produced ranges of computers with futuristic names such as Control Data's 'Cyberdata' series of the 1970s, and the Sinclair home computers

Ferranti Pegasus, 1956.

A Ferranti Orion installation, 1963.

The console of the IBM SSEC, 1948. Was science fiction inspired by computer consoles, or were computer consoles inspired by science fiction?

'ZX80' and 'ZX81' received the 'ZX' prefix purely for the same futuristic, advanced technology connotations of the letters. Various stories are told about the naming of the early home computer, the 'Altair 8800', named after an actual star. Some sources say that its creator, Ed Roberts, asked his daughter for a high-tech sounding name, and she suggested Altair, which just happened to be the star being visited by the crew of the *Starship Enterprise* in an episode of *Star Trek* that she was watching at the time.[38] A less inspiring version by the co-founder of the company that made the Altair claims Roberts didn't care what is was called, and that the technical editor of *Popular Electronics*, the magazine it first appeared in, came up with the name because the computer was a 'stellar event'.[39] In addition to science-fiction-sounding product names, many other products were given series numbers that took the name of the manufacturer or their initials followed by huge figures. Hewlett-Packard's HP3000 of 1977, BTI Computer Systems BTI5000 of 1979, the Kienzle 6000 of 1975, and Kenrick & Jefferson's MDS9000 Data Entry System of 1977 are examples of product names that connote the advanced power of the machine, or suggest millennial dates far in the future (in the same way that towards the end of the twentieth century, an increasingly large number of new designs of everything from toasters to hi-fi furniture to hospital equipment were labelled 'Concept 2000').

The association with science-fiction-sounding names and the misapprehension that computers had been a long-standing component of science fiction stories may account for a number of assumptions by writers that science fiction had been a major influence on the design of early computers. However, when the representation of computers in popular culture is looked at closely, it becomes apparent that such suggestions are nowhere near as straightforward as it might appear. As described above, computers in film in particular turn out to have been not so much flights of fancy, but far more closely based

on real technological developments extrapolated forward (and sometimes not all that far) merely for effect.

One aspect of early computers that was particularly subject to this view of having been a part of science fiction was the computer console:

> There was a time when console units were only a science fiction illustrator's standby. If a spaceship interior in *Amazing Stories* or a Dan Dare strip looked too bleak, an illustrator would deck it out with vast arrays of glowing lights and dials. Futurists tended to see Earthbound business being conducted from winking, omnipotent consoles too. The console became a cipher for the technological prowess of the corporation to come.[40]

Similarly, the reference to 'console' in the Computer Desktop Encyclopedia[41] shows pictures of IBM and UNIVAC mainframes with the text 'Up until the late 1970s, computers were designed with panels of blinking lights, which added to their aura of science fiction.' So, was the computer console Dan Dare's desk? As has been described, some of the earliest consoles for electronic computers appeared on

Still from *2001: A Space Odyssey*, 1968. Even HAL 9000 had a console similar to computers of the time.

government and military computers in the early 1950s and then on early business machines in the 1950s and '60s as a result of the need to provide a centralized method of programming a computer without having to wander round the machine reconfiguring circuitry to perform a particular function. But consoles themselves were not a new concept. Apart from appearing alongside large-scale electro-mechanical calculators, such as the IBM SSEC, more complex purpose-built consoles had been used for some time, wherever the control of complex electrical processes needed to occur – for example in radio broadcasting or in power stations.[42] Even if viewers did not fully understand the functions or capabilities of computers, the console operating a room of electronic cabinetry would have been recognizable to the public as a computer interface at this point. Large consoles were seen in television documentary reportage on the space race, and started to appear in popular film and television in the late 1950s and early 1960s – in the bunkers of the master criminals in James Bond and *Man from U.N.C.L.E.* movies, and as mentioned, in the films *Desk Set* and *Billion Dollar Brain.* Even HAL,

Still from *Flash Gordon: Space Soldiers,* 1936. Spaceship controls as imagined in the 1930s.

the futuristic, sentient supercomputer of *2001: A Space Odyssey*, despite its ship-wide invisible presence and verbal communication abilities, was given a control console not dissimilar to those of real-world mainframe computers of the day.

As it has been noted that computers did not appear in science fiction before they appeared as real objects, it is problematic to suggest that the designers of early computer consoles based their designs on science fiction illustrations. The suggestion that computer consoles appeared in Dan Dare before they did in reality is patently untrue, but it points to some confusion or misinterpretation of what exactly was being portrayed in science fiction imagery. The consoles of spaceships appearing in early science fiction illustrations and films, with their screens, dials, lights and levers, were not about computing at all, but about the control of the vehicles and a connection to the environments outside of them. It is more than likely that man's ability to travel to the ends of the earth by ship, submarine and in particular

McBride wanted to get home in a hurry. There was a spaceship available, but an experimental model that wouldn't work, it didn't have a pilot, and the only pilot around didn't have a license!

Illustration from *Astounding Science Fiction*, 1944.

the aeroplane after the start of the twentieth century fuelled the imaginations of science fiction writers and illustrators contemplating travelling between the stars, and the instrument-crowded cockpits, bridges and helms of these vehicles would have provided an obvious starting point for projecting forward and expanding such controls to fill the flight decks of interplanetary spacecraft. As such, the consoles of science fiction were extrapolations of existing developments in *instrumentation* rather than futuristic predictions of *computing*.

While the influence of Dan Dare (or similar stories) on the design of early computer consoles is at best questionable, the case for the influence of science fiction or at least the zeitgeist of the space race on the designed form of the computer terminal from the late 1950s into the 1970s becomes far more convincing. Space-related aspects

Sperry-Rand UNIVAC 1107, 1961.

of popular culture had elements of the unknown and an air of un-certainty associated with them, and they provided a fertile breeding ground for diversity, imagination and new forms in all areas of de-sign. There is an easy alliance to be seen between the computer's role as forward-looking technology and the futuristic fantasy of science fiction. An excellent example of this influence can be seen in Mario Bellini's TCV 250 computer terminal for Olivetti designed in 1967, which was stated in a retrospective exhibition catalogue to have 'a science fiction aspect'.[43] And by the mid-1970s, a science fiction (or at the very least a 'space race' influence) can be seen in the designs of computer terminals such as the Lear Siegler ADM-2 ('the second generation of the American Dream Machine'!), with its 'docking' key-board, recalling the joining of landing modules to space rockets seen in broadcasts of the missions to the moon, or the combined monitors and keyboards housed in flowing, curvilinear casings produced by a number of different companies. The NCR Criterion integrated a

Dan Dare's desk: like many others of the period, Mario Bellini's 1967 TCV 250 computer terminal for Olivetti displayed a clear science fiction influence.

ADM-2

By customer demand the second generation of the American Dream Machine
(ADM-2) is now available. It provides the
user with flexibility of format, security,
editing, interface, and transmission.

features

- Full 128 ASCII character set
- 1920 Character display
- 8 Transmission rates
- 16 Function keys for 32 commands
- 8 Status displays on the screen

specifications

CRT
12" Diagonal
P4 Phosphor (white) etched faceplate

DISPLAYED CHARACTER SET
128 character ASCII upper and lower case

CURSOR MO
→ ◄ ◄ ↑
HOME, TAB

NUMERIC KE
0 - 9 . T
shift.

variety of computer components into a white, seamless surface, which looked as if it could have come straight from the flight deck of the *Starship Enterprise* in *Star Trek*. This integration of components into a single surface, as seen in the Olivetti and NCR examples, was a recurring metaphor for advanced technology in product designs of the time, the continuously flowing surfaces seen as evidence of 'techno-logical design utopias dreamed up in the seventies, drafts for a world in which what had once been science fiction would become reality.'[44]

The texts accompanying these images in the brochures, heavily concerned as they were with the future expandability and upgrade-ability of expensive hardware, promised 'compatibility not only from model to model, but from generation to generation'.[45] Such sentiments point to another justification for such forward-looking, futuristic styling, as it was (mistakenly) assumed that individual machines would be around for a significant length of time, and therefore could not afford to appear in any way old-fashioned.

Lear Siegler ADM-2, 1975.

The NCR Criterion.

The NCR Criterion is the first of a completely new series of computers that set a standard for productivity and value for money.

The Criterion is a 'virtual' machine. That is, it changes characteristics to fit each job.

Simply by loading a discette it can become a 'virtual' system, for example, for COBOL 74, dynamic multi-programming or an NCR Century.

So the Criterion has great flexibility and a broad range of usability.

With this new system, NCR continues to offer the highest degree of compatibility not only from model to model, but from generation to generation.

Furthermore, the Criterion reduces operating costs by providing the power of a large-scale system in a compact package. It is extraordinarily fast–up to 56 nanoseconds processor cycle time.

It also offers virtual storage, making programming easier and more flexible. Modular growth without processor replacement. Greater on-line programme capability. Expandable memory–128K to one megabyte. And extensive peripheral mixes to meet your needs. More reasons why we say the Criterion sets a new standard for productivity.

NCR Document Processing Terminal, 1974.

NCR Criterion, 1976.

One of the most 'space age' and futuristically styled designs of all computers looked like something NASA might have produced for one of the Apollo space rockets, and would not have looked out of place on the set of *2001: A Space Odyssey*. The CRAY series of super-computers came in a range of bright colours, and were as far from the rational, Bauhaus-inspired boxes of IBM computers as it was possible to get. The first of the series, the CRAY-1 of 1976, was 'a hollow, 16-sided column, 6½ feet tall, nearly five feet wide, and surrounded by upholstered benches'.[46] It weighed five tons and cost $8 million. The circular form reduced the distance between connections, enabling the machine to run faster. It could perform a staggering 80 million calculations per second – ten times faster than the most advanced machines of its competitors. The upholstered benches contained the computer's enormous power supplies and cooling systems, with one reviewer highlighting their scale by comparing the machine's power

CRAY-1 Supercomputer, 1976. Looking more like a part of the Apollo space rocket, the CRAY-1 consumed ten times as much power as Skylab.

consumption of 100Kw with that of the Skylab space station's meagre 10Kw.[47] The CRAY-1 generated so much heat in use, that when Cray Research opened a software facility in a large unheated warehouse in Minnesota, they had no need of a heating system, even in the middle of winter![48] The machine's heat had to be carried away by stainless steel tubes filled with Freon refrigerant. This meant it had no requirement for its own air-conditioned room, but it did project a somewhat ethereal image of a machine that had its own circulatory system.

CRAY supercomputers are a rare example of computer hardware associated with a single individual. Seymour Cray founded Cray Research Inc. in 1973 after working for Sperry-Rand's UNIVAC division and then Control Data Corporation, where he designed some of the fastest and most powerful computers available. Anecdotally,

CRAY-2 Supercomputer, 1981.

when asked what CAD tools he used to design the CRAY-1, he said #3 pencils and quadrille pads. When he was told that Apple had just bought a CRAY to help design the next Mac, Cray replied that he had just bought a Mac to design the next CRAY![49]

By the time of the emergence of personal computers in the late 1970s and their wide popularity in the early 1980s, the link between computers and science fiction was even more firmly established. As domestic objects, home computers were less restricted in their appearance than business machines and consequently were even more able to be presented as space-age objects. This association was reinforced by the widespread usage of home computers for video gaming, as, since their introduction, a large number of computer games had had space-related themes. They could also be presented more freely in technically associated colours such as white, black and silver,

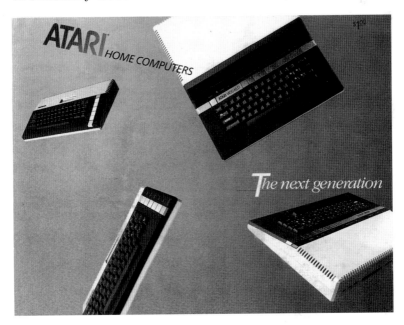

Atari XL Home Computers brochure, 1983. The home computer became a white, angular space-age object.

whereas the dominance and persistence of IBM PC and its clones had by this point made desktop machines in the workplace universally beige. Numerous manufacturers raced to get new products to market in order to cash in on the boom in home computing, which for the most part consisted of self-contained, angular units in sharply detailed plastic cases. As one commentator wrote:

> Designers approached the first personal computers with the science fiction models of *Buck Rogers* and *2001* fixed firmly in their minds. Those images – visions of what a computer would look like if it existed – inspired the shape the machine took when it finally became a reality.[50]

The 1977 Commodore PET 2001 and the 1980 Sinclair ZX80 were the best-selling examples of home computers presented in futuristic-looking angular cases of white plastic, bearing ultra-modern membrane keypads to reflect 'space-age technology'. The connotations of these computers to futuristic space travel were strongly reinforced by their accompanying promotional images, which portrayed them as spaceships, orbiting the Earth, or silently floating through an endless void. Commodore even hired the captain of the *Starship Enterprise*, the actor William Shatner, to promote their products in television commercials (later, Time Computers were to hire Spock – the actor Leonard Nimoy). Similarly, the 1979 Texas Instruments TI-99/4 arrived in a sharply angled 'high-tech' silver casing and betrayed another 'space-race' connection in using software programs supplied in solid-state, plug-in units called 'Command Modules'.

These forms of home computers reflected a level of excitement about computers as products that is clearly no longer present. At the start of the 1980s, over 30 years after the ENIAC was so proudly announced to the world, the electronic computer still held the capacity to electrify its audience. Whether it was a desktop PC that could enable

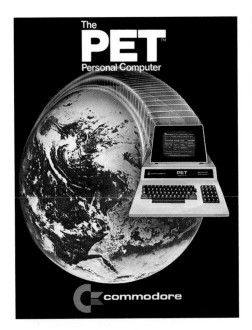

Commodore PET 2001, 1977.

Sinclair ZX80, 1980.

Texas Instruments TI-99/4A, 1981.

a week's work to be completed in a few minutes, or a home computer that allowed a teenager to blast creatures from another planet into oblivion, the computer as an object firmly held people's attention. Over the course of the 1980s, however, this position changed dramatically. As the cost of technology reduced and the number of computers being manufactured increased, their familiarity grew and their novelty waned. The electronic computer had, over the course of its history, diversified from a mainframe computer that filled a whole room with cabinets of cold steel into a whole range of different forms that inspired admiration and commanded respect. Computers and their terminals had taken the form of futuristic consoles and purpose-built desks; monitors appeared and displayed computer code, giving their operators a visual glimpse into the abstract binary universe of the machine's internal workings. Even when the technology reached a point where stand-alone computers could be placed on desktops across the office, they took myriad diverse appearances reflecting their inherent differences and intended audiences. Then, far more rapidly than the computer had developed into so many different objects, standardization set in with a vengeance. As computers came to understand the same language and share the same operating system, they also started to share the same appearance. Technical compatibility came coupled with stylistic similarity, and the designed form of the desktop computer became a given. Following the widespread adoption of the IBM PC, computers quickly moved from being the very embodiment of futuristic fantasy to being 'graceless, lumpy objects . . . an electronic Model T'.[51] Office computers and home computers became one and the same thing - identical, characterless clones of a bland, uninspiring design, whose 'sheer sameness ought to make us suspicious'.[52] In the face of constant exposure to technological developments and the repetitive image of a boring beige box, it is no wonder that computers no longer instilled any sense of awe in their observers. Where

Babbage's calculating machine had set pulses racing, the Personal Computer became an Indifference Engine – a nondescript piece of equipment met largely with ennui. As such, it no longer took any influence in its styling or any aspect of its design from the iconography of space travel or the futuristic utopias of science fiction, but projected instead the dull, staid world of the office – spaceship flight decks and space rocket engines replaced as inspiration by photocopiers and filing cabinets. Despite being continually replaced as they became technologically obsolete, the required perception that the new machine would take over where the old one left off meant that there was no requirement for the kind of stylistic obsolescence found in other consumer products. The desk-bound computer had become a stylistic dead end. Even when Apple decided to stop producing computers that were visually identical to the IBM PC and launched the revolutionary Apple iMac, they struggled to topple its monopoly. Any excitement about the computer itself was to be found instead in the more status-ridden and visually demanding world of mobile computing. Yet even here, the business requirements that had instigated the successful briefcase-inspired laptop computer proved to be difficult to overcome. The possibilities for redesigning the laptop proved to be limited, as again, its designed form had become a given.

There remains, though, a constant drive for the latest technology, which is still a cause for excitement. Handheld devices (combining portable computing, web access, media recording and playback along with email, text and voice communication) are the current battleground for companies desperately fighting to win a share of a ready market, and their launch events are still front-page news. But when the end product is no more than a touch-sensitive screen, whither design? The answer, of course, lies in the design of the interaction. Computers have always been completely reliant on their software in order to be of any use, but the concentration of design effort on the usability of that software is a surprisingly recent phenomenon. The move away from text-based user interfaces to Graphical User Interfaces developed during the 1970s was the first step in this direction, but GUIs only really became significant to users in the mid-1980s with Apple's Macintosh Operating System and became the norm in the early 1990s with Microsoft's Windows 3.0. From this point on, it was the quality of the experience of using the software rather than the hardware that was of interest to most. As one computer historian put it, 'the operating system is the identity of the computer, the personality of the computer. What's the name on it? IBM, Compaq, Dell, Gateway, Acorn – who cares?'[53] This is obviously not the case with the many Mac fans out there, but even when the design of a particular product is highly feted, as in the almost religious fervour surrounding the Apple iPhone (they're not called 'Macolytes' for nothing!), customers eagerly await reviews of the interaction experience. Does it take ages to load up and start? Are programs clunky or temperamental, or a pleasure to use? In the case of the iPhone, a huge proportion of interest in the product has been around its online App Store, where third-party applications can be downloaded to personalize the product's capabilities.[54] The content, not the object, is now the real centre of attention.

As might be expected over such a long time period, representations of computers in popular culture have been diverse. This reflects our relationship with computing technology, which too has been complex and varied. One of the few consistencies is that computers have always been seen as agents of change, whether that change has been for better or worse. With respect to the effects of the representations of computers on their design, it cannot be convincingly argued that they had a significant impact on the form the computer took on its first appearance, but clearly, science fiction and the imagery of the space race played a key part in the later design of computers. It is not being suggested, however, that it was only the design of computers that bore

such influences. As a commercial product, the computer was subject to the majority of stylistic vagaries that affected any other designed artefacts, and the influence of this type of imagery on design could be seen in myriad products of the period, not just technological ones. It was, however, particularly pertinent to the design of computers. Their status as constantly improving, cutting-edge developments at a time of rapidly changing technological advances in many walks of life explains the adoption of space-race and science fiction imagery as appropriate points of reference for the styling of computer products between the 1960s and 1980s; although from that point onward, as they quickly became everyday items, the role of the computer as an embodiment of the future was finally made redundant.

Apple iPad, 2010. When the computer ceased to be an embodiment of the future, all attention turned to the content.

References

Introduction

1 Steven Levy, *Insanely Great: The Life and Times of Macintosh, the Computer that Changed Everything* (London, 1994), p. 13.
2 Michael Williams, 'A Preview of Things to Come: Some Remarks on the First Generation of Computers', in *The First Computers: History and Architectures*, ed. Raúl Rojas and Ulf Hashagen (Cambridge, MA, 2000).
3 See, for example, Paul E. Ceruzzi, *A History of Modern Computing*, 2nd edn (Cambridge, MA, 2003).
4 David Caminer et al., *The World's First Business Computer: User-Driven Innovation* (London, 1996).
5 The 'traditional' generational model of computing development appears in numerous places in slightly different forms. An early example of a four generation model appeared in *Computers '66: An Annual Survey of the Computer Industry in Britain* (Croydon, 1966), p. 17, where the third generation was a faster version of the second, and the fourth generation included the use of integrated circuits.
6 William Aspray and Donald DeB. Beaver, 'Marketing the Monster: Advertising Computer Technology', *Annals of the History of Computing*, VIII/2 (April 1986), pp. 127–43.
7 Ceruzzi, *A History of Modern Computing*, p. 6.

1 Polar Positions

1 Babbage's design intended to use cards similar to those employed on Joseph-Marie Jacquard's weaving loom of 1804, in which the pattern to be produced was controlled by holes cut into wooden cards which determined the lifting of warp threads for each pass of the shuttle.
2 Although I am principally referring here to the debates about the concept of the

stored program computer between Alan Turing and John von Neumann (see below), Louise Purbrick also notes the extent to which Babbage has been praised so much for a conceptual machine which was never realized. She asks: 'If a machine has value regardless of function, what kind of object is a machine?' Louise Purbrick, 'The Dream Machine: Charles Babbage and His Imaginary Computers', *Journal of Design History*, VI/1 (1993), p. 14.

3　Ibid., p. 21.

4　Charlie Gere, *Digital Culture* (London, 2002), p. 25.

5　Tommy Flowers quoted in Michael Smith, *Station X* (London, 2004), p. 157.

6　Barbara Abernethy quoted in Smith, *Station X*, p. 36.

7　Tommy Flowers quoted in Smith, *Station X*, p. 156.

8　Ibid.

9　Due to the circumstances surrounding their production and the fact that these were all for the same client for the same purpose, the Colossus has not been considered here as a computer specifically designed to be serially produced.

10　Simon Singh, *The Science of Secrecy: The Secret History of Codes and Codebreaking* (London, 2000), p. 131 and Smith, *Station X*, Acknowledgements.

11　Smith, *Station X*, p. 206.

12　Simon Lavington, *Early British Computers* (Manchester, 1980), p. 25.

13　Anthony E. Sale, 'The Colossus of Bletchley Park – The German Cipher System', in *The First Computers: History and Architectures*, ed. Raúl Rojas and Ulf Hashagen (Cambridge, MA, 2000), p. 362.

14　Martin Campbell-Kelly, *The Computer Age* (Hove, 1978), p. 54.

15　Arthur W. Burks, 'Electronic Computing Circuits of the ENIAC', *Proceedings of the IRE*, vol. XXXV/8 (1947), p. 756.

16　Anon, 'An Electronic Brain', *The Times*, Friday 1 November 1946, p. 2.

17　Ibid., p. 57.

18　Apparently, von Neumann 'repeatedly emphasized the fundamental conception [of a stored program computer] was Turing's': B. Jack Copeland and Diane Proudfoot, 'Turing and the Computer', in *Alan Turing's Automatic Computing Engine*, ed. B. Jack Copeland (Oxford, 2005), p. 114.

19　Mercury delay lines were developed for use with RADAR systems as a means of temporarily storing information. Information was introduced into physical tubes of mercury in the form of electrical pulses, and the waves created travelled through the tube. At the other end the pulses were retrieved, amplified and re-introduced to the tube, so refreshing the information indefinitely.

20　Referred to as 'von Neumann Architecture' despite the input of his colleagues.

21　B. Jack Copeland, 'The Origins and Development of the ACE Project', in *Alan Turing's Automatic Computing Engine*, ed. Copeland, p. 58.

22　Donald W. Davies, Foreword to *Alan Turing's Automatic Computing Engine*, ed. Copeland, p. viii.

23　As with mercury delay lines, the notion of using cathode ray tubes (CRTs) as memory devices came from RADAR developments. Using CRTs, electrical pulses appeared as dots and dashes, and the charges at the gaps between them on the screen were recorded and put back into the system in the same way as with delay lines, recreating the original pattern.

24 Campbell-Kelly, *The Computer Age*, p. 50.
25 IBM Archives available online at www-03.ibm.com/ibm/history/reference/faq_ 0000000011.html (accessed 8 November 2008).
26 Tom Vickers, 'Applications of the Pilot ACE and the DEUCE', in *Alan Turing's Automatic Computing Engine*, ed. Copeland, p. 269.
27 Anon, 'Biggest Electronic Brain in Europe', *The Times*, Thursday 16 May 1957, p. 11.
28 Vickers, 'Applications of the Pilot ACE and the Duece', p. 268.
29 B. Jack Copeland, in the Introduction to *Alan Turing's Automatic Computing Engine*, ed. Copeland, p. 4.
30 Emerson W. Pugh and William Aspray, 'Creating the Computer Industry', *IEEE Annals of the History of Computing*, vol. XVIII/2 (1996), pp. 7–17.
31 Ibid., p. 7.
32 Ibid., p. 8.
33 As Paul Ceruzzi notes, 'just as it helped inaugurate modern data processing in 1890 by working with Herman Hollerith, [using the punched-card tabulator] the Census also helped electronic computing's transition from the university to the private sector.' Paul Cerruzi, *A History of Modern Computing*, 2nd edn (Cambridge, MA, 2003), p. 26.
34 JoAnne Yates, 'The Structuring of Early Computer Use in Life Insurance', *Journal of Design History*, XII/1 (1999), p. 13.
35 Cerruzi, *A History of Modern Computing*, p. 30.
36 Harry D. Huskey, 'Test Assembly, Pilot ACE, Big ACE, and Bendix G-15', in *Alan Turing's Automatic Computing Engine*, ed. Copeland, p. 290.
37 B. Jack Copeland, in the Introduction to *Alan Turing's Automatic Computing Engine*, ed. Copeland, p. 5.
38 *Fortune*, July 1955, cited in Ceruzzi, *A History of Modern Computing*, p. 57.
39 Eliot Noyes, speech at Hastings Hall, Yale, Connecticut, 8 December 1976. Cited in Gordon Bruce, *Eliot Noyes: A Pioneer of Design and Architecture in the Age of American Modernism* (New York, 2006), p. 146.
40 Harry D. Huskey, 'SWAC: The Pioneer Day Session at NCC July 1978', in *The Annals of the History of Computing*, IX/2 (1997), pp. 51–61.
41 Sibylle Kircherer, *Olivetti: A Study of the Corporate Management of Design* (London, 1990), p. 16.
42 John Heskett, *Industrial Design* (London, 1980), p. 140.
43 Gianni Barbacetto, *Design Interface: How Man and Machine Communicate. Olivetti Design Research by King and Miranda* (Milan, 1987), p. 18.
44 Kircherer, *Olivetti*, p. 39.
45 Ibid., p. 42.
46 Ettore Sottsass, cited in Kircherer, *Olivetti*, p. 42.

47 Ettore Sottsass in an interview with Lorena Muñoz-Alonso, October 2006, available online at: http://selfselector.co.uk/2007/03/28/meeting-mr-sottsass/. Accessed 9 November 2009.

48 Kircherer, *Olivetti*, p. 42.

49 Penny Sparke, *Ettore Sottsass Jr.* (London, 1982), p. 42.

50 Thomas Watson Jr and Peter Petre, *Father, Son and Co.: My Life at IBM and Beyond* (New York, 1990), p. 259. Cited in Bruce, *Eliot Noyes,* p. 154.

51 Emerson Pugh and William Aspray, 'Creating the Computer Industry', *IEEE Annals of the History of Computing*, XVIII/2 (1996), p. 15.

52 Campbell-Kelly, *The Computer Age*, p. 86.

53 Pugh and Aspray, 'Creating the Computer Industry', p. 15.

54 John Heskett, *Industrial Design* (London, 1980), p. 141.

55 The full story of this remarkable institution is told in great detail in Michael Hiltzik, *Dealers of Lightning: Xerox PARC and the Dawn of the Computer Age* (London, 2000).

56 Jay P. Pederson, ed., *International Directory of Company Histories, Vol. 26* (Detroit, MI, 1999), p. 543.

57 Hiltzik, *Dealers of Lightning*, p. 29.

58 Ibid., p. 45.

59 Ibid., p. 49.

60 Logitech Inc., *Douglas C. Engelbart: A Profile of His Work and Vision: Past, Present and Future*, unpublished report (Oct. 2005).

61 Andries van Dam, speaking at 'Engelbart and the Dawn of Interactive Computing', an event held at Stanford University, 9 December 2008, to mark the 40th anniversary of the 1968 demo. Available online at: www.sri.com/engvideos/panel1.html. Accessed 9 November 2009.

62 Interview with Doug Engelbart at the headquarters of Logitech Inc., Fremont, California, 10 April 2006.

63 Ibid.

64 Logitech Inc., *The Computer Mouse: Adapting Computers to Human Needs: The Evolution of Computer Pointing Devices*, unpublished report (Aug. 1993).

65 Hiltzik, *Dealers of Lightning*, p. 166.

66 Ibid., p. 203.

67 Ibid., p. 79.

68 Ibid., p. 206.

69 The first email using the now ubiquitous '@' symbol as a domain separator was sent by Ray Tomlinson over the ARPANET in 1971.

70 Hiltzik, *Dealers of Lightning*, p. 209.

71 Ibid., p. 264.

72 See, for example, Douglas K. Smith and Robert C. Alexander, *Fumbling the Future: How Xerox Invented, Then Ignored, the First Personal Computer* (New York, 1988). See also Hiltzik, *Dealers of Lightning*, passim.

73 Steve Jobs, quoted in Hiltzik, *Dealers of Lightning*, p. 389.

74 Steven Levy, *Insanely Great: The Life and Times of Macintosh, the Computer That Changed Everything* (London, 1995), p. 70.
75 Hiltzik, *Dealers of Lightning*, p. 366.
76 Paul Kunkel, *Apple Design: The Work of the Apple Industrial Design Group* (New York, 1997), p. 18.
77 A detailed description of this work can be seen in the form of primary documentation in the online archive from Stanford University, 'Making the Macintosh, Technology and Culture in Silicon Valley'. (http://library.stanford.edu/mac/, accessed 1 August 2006).
78 A. S. Pang, 'The Making of the Mouse', in *American Heritage of Invention and Technology*, XVIII/3 (Winter 2002), p. 49.
79 Rickson Sun, interview with Dennis Boyle, Jim Yurchenco, and Rickson Sun at the offices of IDEO, Palo Alto, California, 7 April 2006.
80 Hovey-Kelly chose to accept a flat fee for Yurchenco's mouse design instead of a royalty, unaware that it 'would serve as the core technology for millions of mice produced in the years to come', Kunkel, *Apple Design*, p. 20.
81 Jim Yurchenco, interview with Dennis Boyle, Jim Yurchenco, and Rickson Sun at the offices of IDEO, Palo Alto, California, 7 April 2006.
82 Kunkel, *Apple Design*, p. 20.
83 Among these are Steven Levy, *Insanely Great: The Life and Times of Macintosh, the Computer that Changed Everything* (London, 1995); Andy Hertzfeld, *Revolution in the Valley: The Insanely Great Story of How The Mac Was Made* (Sebastopol, CA, 2005); and Steve Wozniak and Gina Smith, *iWoz. Computer Geek to Cult Icon: How I Invented the Personal Computer, Co-founded Apple, and Had Fun Doing It* (New York, 2006).
84 Levy, *Insanely Great*, p. 4.
85 Kunkel, *Apple Design*, p. 46.
86 Levy, *Insanely Great*, p. 140.
87 Dave Brasgalla, quoted in Mark Penfold, 'Design Icon: The Mac Icons', *Computer Arts*, available at: www.computerarts.co.uk/in_depth/features/design_icon_the_mac_icons (accessed 12 December 2008).
88 Mitch Kapor, quoted in Levy, *Insanely Great*, p. 163.
89 Joanna Hoffman, quoted in Levy, *Insanely Great*, p. 186.
90 Mark Frauenfelder, *The Computer: An Illustrated History* (London, 2005), p. 143.

2 Personal Matters

1 Vannevar Bush, 'As we may think', in *The Atlantic Monthly* (July 1945). Available online at http://web.mit.edu/STS.035/www/PDFs/think.pdf, accessed 17 September 2008.
2 Interview with Doug Engelbart at the headquarters of Logitech Inc., Fremont,

California, 10 April 2006.

3 Leslie Haddon, 'The Home Computer: The Making of a Consumer Electronic', *Science as Culture*, II (1988), p. 7.

4 Ibid., p. 27.

5 Leslie Haddon, and David Skinner, 'The Enigma of the Micro: Lessons From the British Home Computer Boom', *Social Science Computer Review*, IX/3 (1991), p. 445.

6 John Markhoff, *What the Dormouse Said: How the Sixties Counter-culture Shaped the Personal Computer Industry* (London, 2005), p. 251.

7 At www.kenbak–1.net/index.htm (accessed 11 September 2008).

8 Jonathan A. Titus, 'Computer!', *Mark-8 Construction Booklet* (1974), p. 15. Available online at: http://bytecollector.com/m8_docs.htm. Accessed 10 November 2009.

9 Frank Delaney, *History of the Microcomputer Revolution*, transcript of radio series, KPBX Radio (1995). Available online at: www.virtualaltair.com/virtualaltair.com/mits0015.asp, accessed 11 June 2004.

10 Paul Kunkel, *Apple Design: The Work of the Apple Industrial Design Group* (New York, 1997) p. 12.

11 Haddon, *The Home Computer*, p. 14.

12 Steve Wozniak and Gina Smith, *iWoz. Computer Geek to Cult Icon: How I Invented the Personal Computer, co-founded Apple, and Had Fun Doing It* (New York, 2006), p. 188.

13 Justin Hall in Van Burnham, *Supercade: A Visual History of the Videogame Age 1971–1974* (Cambridge, MA, 2001), p. 156.

14 Steven Levy, *Insanely Great: The Life and Times of Macintosh, the Computer that Changed Everything* (London, 1995), p. 134.

15 Markhoff, *What the Dormouse Said*, p. 282.

16 Stephen Wozniak, 'Homebrew and how the Apple came to be', in Steve Ditlea, (1984) *Digital Deli*, posted on www.atariarchives.org/deli/index.php, accessed 18 August 2008.

17 Anon, 'In the year 2001, the shape of everyday things . . .', in *Esquire* (May 1966), p. 116.

18 Alan Kay, email communication to the author, 8 August 2007.

19 Alan Kay and A. Goldberg, 'Personal Dynamic Media', *Computing*, X/3 (March 1977), pp. 31–41, 31. This is a condensed version of the original Learning Research Group Technical Report SSL-76-1 in *Personal Dynamic Media* (Xerox PARC, Palo Alto, CA, April 1976).

20 I. Stobie, 'They all laughed, but . . .', in *Practical Computing* (January 1983), p. 108.

21 Email communication with Alan Kay, 31 August 2008.

22 Robert Slater, *Portraits in Silicon* (Cambridge, MA, 1987), p. 323.

23 M. Aartsen, 'Portable computers, a buyer's guide', in *Design* (March 1984), p. 48.

24 Interviews with John Ellenby by telephone and email, February 2001.

25 'The Compass Computer: The Design Challenges Behind the Innovation', in *Innovation – The Journal of the Industrial Designers Society of America*, (Winter 1983), pp. 4–8.

26 At http://laptop.org/en/vision/progress/index.shtml, accessed 18 January 2008.

27 Clint Witchalls, 'Bridging the Digital Divide', *The Guardian* Online Section, 17 February 2005, p. 24.

28 Kate Bevan, 'Are One Laptop Per Child Sales Living Up to Expectations?', *The Guardian* (Technology Section), 29 November 2007, p. 2.

29 Jack Schofield, 'The Sugar Daddy for Future Generations', *The Guardian* Technology Section, 29 January 2009, p. 5.

30 Barbara Buell and Richard Brandt, 'The Pen: Computing's Next Big Leap', *Business Week*, 14 May 1990.

31 Ivan E. Sutherland, *Sketchpad, A Man-Machine Graphical Communication System* (PhD. thesis, MIT, January 1963). Available online at: www.cl.cam.ac.uk/techreports/UCAM-CL-TR-574.pdf, accessed 6 June 2007.

32 Computer History Museum archive: item reference X450.84.

33 Tom O. Ellis, J. F. Heafner, and W. L. Sibley, *The GRAIL Language and Operations* (Memorandum RM-6001-ARPA, Sept. 1969, p. 3) Available online at: www.rand.org/pubs/research_memoranda/2006/RM6001.pdf, accessed 13 June 2007.

34 Samuel Hurst, email communication to the author, 5 July 2007.

35 Peter Muller, email communication to the author, 5 July 2007.

36 Ralph Sklarew, email communication to the author, 5 July 2007.

37 Linus Technologies' patents were later acquired by GRiD Systems after they were sold to Tandy. Available online at http://blinkenlights.com/classiccmp/linus/, accessed 3 July 2007.

38 Interview with Jeff Hawkins at the offices of Numenta, Palo Alto, CA, 10 May 2007.

39 Jerry Kaplan, *Startup: A Silicon Valley Adventure* (New York, 1994), p. 15.

40 Ibid., p. 294.

41 Andy Reinhardt, 'Momenta Points to the Future', *BYTE*, XVI/12 (1991), pp. 48–9.

42 Bill Breen, 'Fresh Start 2002: Starting Over . . . and Over . . . ', *Fast Company*, 54 (2001) p. 77.

43 Joe Wilcox, 'IBM's ThinkPad turns 10', CNET News.com, 6 October 2002. Available online at http://news.cnet.com/IBMs-ThinkPad-turns-10/2100-1040_3-960927.html, accessed 29 August 2008.

44 Kunkel, *Apple Design*, p. 74.

45 Celeste Baranski, email communication to the author, 22 June 2007.

46 Jeff Hawkins, email communication to the author, 24 January 2007.

47 Interview with Jeff Hawkins at the offices of Numenta, Palo Alto, CA, 10 May 2007.

48 Conrad H. Blickenstorfer, '10 Years of Pen Computing', in *Pen Computing Magazine* 50 (June 2004).

49 Michael Kanellos, 'Sony Phasing Out Pen-tablet PCs', available online at http://news.com.com/2100-1040-816422.html, accessed 31 January 2007.

50 Interview with Stuart Card at Palo Alto Research Center, Palo Alto, CA, 9 May 2007.

51 The term 'Personal Digital Assistant' was coined by the CEO of Apple, John Sculley, at the Consumer Electronics Show in Las Vegas, Nevada, January 1993. Available online at http://encyclopedia.thefreedictionary.com/, accessed 4 July 2007.

52 Interview with Jeff Hawkins at the offices of Numenta Inc., Menlo Park, California, 7 April 2006.

53 Ibid.

54 Ibid. Xerox PARC had filed a patent for a similar system designed by David Goldberg called *Unistrokes* a year earlier in 1995 which was granted in 1997. Xerox then successfully sued Palm.

55 Ibid.

56 'Confused? So is everyone else as phones become more like personal digital assistants and PDAs take on more of the functions of phones': Victor Keegan, 'Blackberrys are not the only fruit', in *The Guardian*, Technology Guardian section, 28 June 2006, p. 4.

3 Power Tools

1 William Aspray and Donald deB. Beaver, 'Marketing the Monster: Advertising Computer Technology', *IEEE Annals of the History of Computing*, VIII/2 (1986), p. 138.

2 Juliet Webster, 'From the Word Processor to the Micro: Gender Issues in the Development of Information Technology in the Office', in *Gendered by Design? Information Technology and Office Systems*, ed. E. Green, J. Owen and D. Pain (London, 1993), p. 119.

3 Alan Delgado, *The Enormous File: A Social History of the Office* (London, 1979), pp. 37–8.

4 Ada Lovelace helped Charles Babbage with the theoretical work behind his analytical engine in the 1840s, and in the 1940s Adele Goldstine co-authored important papers in the development of ENIAC, while Grace Hopper developed easier methods of programming computers using a compiler and the COBOL programming language.

5 Harry Polachek, 'Before the ENIAC', *IEEE Annals of the History of Computing*, XVIV/2 (1997), p. 25.

6 Gill Kirkup, 'The Social Construction of Computers: Hammers or Harpsichords?' in G. Kirkup, and L. S. Keller, ed., *Inventing Women: Science, Technology and Gender* (Cambridge, 1992), p. 269.

7 Webster, 'From the Word Processor to the Micro', p. 114.

8 Ibid., p. 113.

9 Ibid., p. 118.

10 Kenrick and Jefferson Ltd, *Keyboard Training* brochure (1977).

11 T. Lindsay, 'Small Screen, Big Style', *Design* (May 1981), p.43.

12 Steve Lubar, *InfoCulture* (Boston, MA, 1993), p. 324.

13 IBM 5100 portable computer brochure, 1976.

14 Kode Ltd, *Central Data Entry System* brochure, 1976.

15 In the US, gender equality and equal pay were incorporated in the Civil Rights Act of 1964. In the UK, these issues were addressed in the Equal Pay Act 1970 and the Sex Discrimination Act of 1975.

16 Apple Computer Inc., *Macintosh Manual* (San Francisco, CA, 1984), p. 13.

17 Gordon McComb, *Macintosh User's Guide* (Indianapolis, IN, 1984), pp. 32–3.

18 Tim Stanton, 'From Our Maus to Baumaus: Logitech vs. Microsoft', in *PC Magazine* (16 February 1988), p. 202. This, too, was in a section called 'Alternate Input Devices', indicating that the mouse was in no way the preferred primary input method at this point.

19 See Mary Douglas and Baron Isherwood, *The World of Goods: Towards an Anthropology of Consumption* (New York, 1979) and Daniel Miller, *Material Culture and Mass Consumption* (Oxford, 1987).

20 Michael Shamberg, 'The Handy Uses of a Home Computer', *Life* (January 1970), p. 49.

21 Ibid.

22 Kirkup, 'The Social Construction of Computers', p. 271.

23 Leslie Haddon, 'Researching Gender and Home Computers' in *Technology and Everyday Life: Trajectories and Transformations*, ed. K. Sørensen and A. Berg (Trondheim, 1990), available at www.mot.chalmers.se/dept/tso/haddon/ GenderPC.pdf (accessed 5 Feb 2008), p. 6.

24 John Markoff, *What the Dormouse Said: How the Sixties Counter-culture Shaped the Personal Computer Industry* (New York, 2005), p. ix.

25 Nick Montford in Van Burnham, *Supercade: A Visual History of the Videogame Age 1971–1974* (Cambridge, MA, 2001), p. 39.

26 Ibid..

27 Van Burnham, *Supercade*, p. 52.

28 Ibid., p. 87.

29 Steve Bloom, 'The First Golden Age', in *Digital Deli*, ed. Steve Ditlea (New York, 1984) available at www.atariarchives.org/deli/golden_age.php (accessed 15 Jan 2009).

30 Leslie Haddon and David Skinner, 'The Enigma of the Micro: Lessons from the British Home Computer Boom', *Social Science Computer Review*, XIV/3 (1991), p. 439.

31 Ibid., p. 442.

32 Greg Williams, 'Microcomputing, British Style: The Fifth Personal Computer World Show', in *Byte* (January 1983), p. 40.

33 Ibid., p. 42.

34 Ibid.

35 Ibid., p. 44.

36 Acorn Computers Ltd, *The Electron User Guide* (Cambridge, 1983), p. 1.
37 See, for example, Roger Silverstone and Eric Hirsch, eds, *Consuming Technologies* (London, 1992), passim.
38 Elaine Lally, *At Home with Computers* (Oxford, 2002), p. 167.
39 See Grant McCracken, *Culture and Consumption* (Indianapolis, IN, 1988), which describes objects as markers of status and hierarchies of relationships.
40 Mihaly Csikszentmihalyi, and Eugene Rochberg-Halton, *The Meaning of Things: Domestic Symbols and the Self* (Cambridge, 1981), p. 29.
41 Judith Williamson, *Decoding Advertisements: Ideology and Meaning in Advertising* (London, 1978), p. 38.
42 Ibid.
43 Colin Campbell, *The Romantic Ethic and the Spirit of Modern Consumerism* (Oxford, 1987), p. 89.
44 Bill Osgerby, 'So You're the Famous Simon Templar', in *Action TV: Tough Guys, Smooth Operators and Foxy Chicks*, ed. Bill Osgerby and Anna Gough-Yates (London, 2001), p. 44.
45 Reyner Banham, 'Power Plank', *New Society* (28 June 1973). Reprinted in *A Critic Writes: Essays by Reyner Banham*, ed. Mary Banham (California, 1993), p. 184.
46 Associated Press, 'Momenta to Show "Pentop Computer"', *New York Times*, 4 October 1991.
47 'No product since the personal computer has changed corporate life as the Blackberry has. Like it or hate it, most business users ruefully admit that they can't work without it', Victor Keegan, 'Blackberrys are Not the Only Fruit', in *The Guardian*, Technology Guardian section, 28 June 2006, p. 4.
48 Apple MessagePad 2000 brochure APP-BRO–151, March 1997.
49 Polly Curtis, 'Internet Generation Leave Parents Behind', in *The Guardian*, 19 January 2009, p. 4. This article reported on the results of an annual survey which found that 62 per cent of 'five- to 16-year-olds had a social networking site and on average spent 1.7 hours a day online as well as 1.5 hours on games consoles.'
50 When Apple launched the iPhone in the US in July 2007, people queued for days. Apple sold 525,000 units in the first weekend, with most stores selling out within 24 hours. Anon, 'iPhone creates stir on US launch', *BBC News*, 3 July 2007, available online at http://news.bbc.co.uk/1/hi/6260618.stm (accessed 29 September 2009). In the UK, people queued for up to 34 hours. Only 7 per cent of the queue was female. Oliver Burkman, 'At 6.02pm the Worshippers Got Their Reward', in *The Guardian*, 10 November 2007, p. 3.

4 Futuristic Fantasies

1 D. L. Moore, *Ada, Countess of Lovelace, Byron's Illegitimate Daughter* (London, 1977), p. 44.

2 Pierre J. Huss, 'Let's Claim The Moon – Now!', *Mechanix Illustrated* (February 1957), p. 70.

3 T. R. Kennedy Jr, 'Electronic Computer Flashes Answers, May Speed Engineering; New All-Electronic Computer And Its Inventors', *New York Times*, 15 February 1946, p. 1.

4 Linda Sanford, in a speech inducting the ENIAC Programmers into the Women in Technology International (WITI) 1997 Hall of Fame. Speech written by Kathryn A. Kleiman. Available at www.witi.com/center/witimuseum/halloffame/1997/eniac.php, accessed 1 February 2009.

5 Andy Kessler, 'A Colossus Mistake', *Wall Street Wired*, 19 April 2007. Available at http://kessler.blogs.nytimes.com/tag/britain/?scp=12andsq=eniac%201946andst=cse. Accessed 2 February 2009.

6 'Britain to Make a Radio Brain', *Daily Telegraph*, 7 November 1946, reproduced in the Introduction to Jack Copeland, ed., *Alan Turing's Automatic Computing Engine* (Oxford, 2005), p. 6.

7 '"ACE" May Be Fastest Brain', *Daily Telegraph*, 31 January 1950, reproduced in the Introduction to Jack Copeland ed., *Alan Turing's Automatic Computing Engine* (Oxford, 2005), p. 8.

8 Recording of original broadcasting on webpage, Jonathan Fildes, 'Oldest' computer music unveiled, 17 June 2008, available online at http://news.bbc.co.uk/1/hi/technology/7458479.stm. Accessed 6 February 2009.

9 The University of Manchester, 'Oh Baby! First photograph of early modern computer', news item, 17 June 2008. Available at www.manchester.ac.uk/aboutus/news/display/?id=3750. Accessed 6 February 2009.

10 The University of Manchester, 'First Digital Music Made in Manchester', news item, 18 June 2008. Available at www.manchester.ac.uk/aboutus/news/archive/list/item/?id=3754andyear=2008andmonth=06. Accessed 6 February 2009.

11 Jonathan Fildes, '"Oldest" Computer Music Unveiled'.

12 Anon, '8-Foot "Genius" Dedicated; Univac Will Go to Work on Census Bureau's Data', *New York Times*, 15 June 1951, p. 25.

13 Robert K. Plumb, 'Moon Of Jupiter Found By Univac; 8th Satellite, Lost to View Since 1941, Rediscovered by New Calculations', *New York Times*, 24 February 1955, p. 29.

14 Anon, 'Univac Computers To Analyze Beauty', *New York Times*, 20 June 1962, Real Estate section, p. 24.

15 The Associated Press, 'Univac the Brain Unafraid To Be Out on Limb Nov. 4', *New York Times*, 15 October 1952, p. 27.

16 John Alderman, *Core Memory: A Visual Survey of Vintage Computers* (San Francisco, CA, 2007), p. 24.

17 Paul Jennings, news report on the Exhibition of Science, BBC recording from 1951 available online at www.goodeveca.net/nimrod/. Accessed 4 October 2009.

18 This continued a tradition of competing against machines to show the potential of the latest technology. Just over a decade earlier in 1940, a mechanical relay-based

machine called the 'Nimatron', with exactly the same function of playing 'Nim', had been exhibited in the Westinghouse Building of the New York World's Fair. See E. U. Condon, 'The Nimatron', *American Mathematics Monthly* (May 1942), p. 330.

19 Ferranti Ltd., *Faster than Thought: The Ferranti Nimrod Digital Computer*, 1951 Festival of Britain Exhibition booklet. Transcript available at www.goodeveca.net/nimrod/booklet.html. Accessed 2 February 2009.

20 Ferranti Ltd, *Faster than Thought*.

21 Jennings, news report on the Exhibition of Science.

22 Michael Kanellos, 'ENIAC – Monster and Marvel – Debuted 60 Years Ago', *CNET News.com*, 13 February 2006. Available at http://news.cnet.com/2009–1006_3-6037980.htm. Accessed 19 February 2009.

23 Michael Punt, 'Accidental Machines: The Impact of Popular Participation in Computer Technology', *Design Issues*, XIV/1 (1998), pp. 54–80.

24 National Savings and Investments website, at www.nsandi.com/press-room/premiumbonds50/history_pb.jsp. Accessed 3 February 2009.

25 Anon, 'The Brain Builders', *Time*, 28 March 1955, p. 81.

26 Anon., 'Two More Univacs, but There's Still a Need for Additional Clerks', *Home Office* (June 1956), pp. 6–9, cited in JoAnne Yates, 'The Structuring of Early Computer Use in Life Insurance, *Journal of Design History*, XII/1, p. 14.

27 Paul Cerruzi, *A History of Modern Computing*, 2nd edn (Cambridge, MA, 2003), p. 33.

28 William Tenn, 'There Are Robots Among Us', *Popular Electronics* (December 1958), p. 45.

29 Robert Bendiner, 'How Automation Will Affect Your Job', *Mechanix Illustrated*, October 1955, p. 59.

30 David Stubbs, *Genius Gadgets and Gizmos: Weird and Wonderful Contraptions from Yesterday's Future* (London, 2008), p. 18.

31 John Clute, *Science Fiction: The Illustrated Encyclopaedia* (London, 1995), p. 74.

32 Often confused with computer displays, the use of videoscreens in science fiction goes back a lot further than might be imagined, almost to the turn of the nineteenth century, after a cathode ray tube was first used to receive crude images in 1907. Yet despite the capabilities of today's technology, videophones have never been successful. Evidence perhaps of social acceptance being a key factor in technological development.

33 Gordon E. Moore, 'Cramming More Components onto Integrated Circuits', *Electronics*, XXXVIII/8 (19 April 1965).

34 Douglas C. Engelbart, 'Microelectronics and the Art of Similitude', *IEEE International Solid State Circuit Conference Digest of Technical Papers*, III (February 1960), p. 76. Apparently, Gordon Moore, of 'Moore's Law' fame, heard Engelbart give a reading of this 1959 paper at a conference in 1960, five years before he came up with his predictions on computer power.

35 See Christian Wurster, *Computers. An Illustrated History* (Köln, 2002), passim.

36 IBM Corporation Military Products Division with the Department of Defense US Air Force and the Boeing Airplane Company, *On Guard!*, publicity film, c. 1956; Western Electric with the US Air Force, *In Your Defense*, publicity film, c. 1957.

37 Dabbala Rajagopal Reddy, 'An Approach to Computer Speech Recognition by Direct Analysis of the Speech Wave', PhD Thesis, Stanford University, 1966.

38 This story is repeated in numerous places, with an early published source being Annette Milford, 'Computer Power of the Future – The Hobbyists', in *Computer Notes*, I/11 (April 1976), p. 7. Published by MITS on behalf of the Altair Users Group. Available at www.startupgallery.org/gallery/notesViewer.php?ii=76_ 4andp=7. Accessed 27 February 2009.

39 Forrest M. Mims III, 'The Altair Story; Early Days at MITS', *Creative Computing*, X/11 (1984), p. 17.

40 James Woodhuysen, 'Complex Consoles are Coming', *Design* (January 1980), p. 34.

41 At www.computerlanguage.com.

42 The 2008/9 exhibition 'Dan Dare and the Birth of Hi-Tech Britain' at the Science Museum in London placed a control panel from a 1957 Elliot computer near the control console of a power station. Without close scrutiny, it was not easy to tell which was which.

43 Cara McCarty, *Mario Bellini, Designer* (New York, 1987), p. 21.

44 Bernard Busch, cited in Michael Erlhoff, ed., *Designed in Germany since 1949* (München, 1990), p. 147.

45 NCR Critereon Computer brochure, 1976.

46 Jim Schefter, 'Supercomputer', *Popular Science* (June 1979), p. 87.

47 Ibid., p. 88.

48 Charles J. Murray, *The Supermen: The Story of Seymour Cray and the Technical Wizards behind the Supercomputer* (New York, 1997), p. 134.

49 Gordon Bell, 'A Seymour Cray Perspective', Seymour Cray Lecture Series, University of Minnesota, 1997. Available at http://research.microsoft.com/en-us/um/people/gbell/craytalk/sld001.htm. Accessed 28 Feb 2009.

50 Phil Palton, 'The Magic Box', *Connoisseur* (January 1986), p. 55.

51 David Gelernter, *The Aesthetics of Computing* (London, 1988), p. 109.

52 Ibid.

53 Robert X. Cringely in *The Money Programme*, first broadcast by the BBC on 23 March 1997.

54 'The success of products such as the iPhone does not lie in the phone itself but in the applications and services that run through the device.' Oliver Gajda, director of Europe Unlimited, quoted in Michael Pollitt, 'Innovation Nation' in *Media Guardian*, *The Guardian*, 7 September 2009, p. 1.

Select Bibliography

Alderman, John, *Core Memory: A Visual Survey of Vintage Computers* (San Francisco, CA, 2007)

Aspray, William, and Donald DeB. Beaver, 'Marketing the Monster: Advertising Computer Technology', *Annals of the History of Computing*, VIII/2 (April 1986), pp. 127–43

Bruce, Gordon, *Eliot Noyes: A Pioneer of Design and Architecture in the Age of American Modernism* (New York, 2006)

Burnham, Van, *Supercade: A Visual History of the Videogame Age 1971–1974* (Cambridge, MA, 2001)

Caminer, David, et al., *The World's First Business Computer: User-Driven Innovation* (London, 1996)

Campbell-Kelly, Martin, *The Computer Age* (Hove, 1978)

Ceruzzi, Paul E., *A History of Modern Computing*, 2nd edn (Cambridge, MA, 2003)

Copeland, B. Jack, *Alan Turing's Automatic Computing Engine* (Oxford, 2005)

Gere, Charlie, *Digital Culture* (London, 2002)

Green, Eileen, Jenny Owen and Den Pain, *Gendered by Design? Information Technology and Office Systems* (London, 1993)

Haddon, Leslie, 'The Home Computer: The Making of a Consumer Electronic', *Science as Culture*, I/2 (1988), pp. 7–51

—, and David Skinner, 'The Enigma of the Micro: Lessons from the British Home Computer Boom', *Social Science Computer Review*, IX/3 (1991), pp. 435–49

Hertzfeld, Andy, *Revolution in the Valley: The Insanely Great Story of How The Mac Was Made* (Sebastopol, CA, 2005)

Hiltzik, Michael, *Dealers of Lightning: Xerox PARC and the Dawn of the Computer Age* (London, 2000)

Kaplan, Jerry, *Startup: A Silicon Valley Adventure* (New York, 1994)

Kay, Alan, and A. Goldberg, 'Personal Dynamic Media', *Computing*, X/3 (March 1977), pp. 31–41

Kircherer, Sibylle, *Olivetti: A Study of the Corporate Management of Design* (London, 1990)

Kirkup, Gill, and Laurie Smith Keller, *Inventing Women: Science, Technology and Gender* (Cambridge, 1992)

Kunkel, Paul, *Apple Design: The Work of the Apple Industrial Design Group* (New York, 1997)

Lally, Elaine, *At Home with Computers* (Oxford, 2002)

Lavington, Simon, *Early British Computers* (Manchester, 1980)

Levy, Steven, *Insanely Great: The Life and Times of Macintosh, the Computer that Changed Everything* (London, 1994)

Lubar, Steve, *InfoCulture* (Boston, MA, 1993)

Markhoff, John, *What the Dormouse Said: How the Sixties Counter-culture Shaped the Personal Computer Industry* (London, 2005)

Murray, Charles J., *The Supermen: The Story of Seymour Cray and the Technical Wizards behind the Supercomputer* (New York, 1997)

Polachek, Harry, 'Before the ENIAC', *IEEE Annals of the History of Computing*, XIX/2 (1997), pp. 25–30

Pugh, Emerson W., and William Aspray, 'Creating the Computer Industry', *IEEE Annals of the History of Computing*, XVIII/2 (1996), pp. 7–17

Punt, Michael, 'Accidental Machines: The Impact of Popular Participation in Computer Technology', *Design Issues*, XIV/1 (1998), pp. 54–80

Purbrick, Louise, 'The Dream Machine: Charles Babbage and His Imaginary Computers', *Journal of Design History*, VI/1 (1993), p. 14

Rojas, Raúl, and Ulf Hashagen, *The First Computers: History and Architectures* (Cambridge, MA, 2000)

Silverstone, Roger, and Eric Hirsch, *Consuming Technologies* (London, 1992)

Singh, Simon, *The Science of Secrecy: The Secret History of Codes and Codebreaking* (London, 2000)

Slater, Robert, *Portraits in Silicon* (Cambridge, MA, 1987)

Smith, Michael, *Station X* (London, 2004)

Sparke, Penny, *Ettore Sottsass Jr.* (London, 1982)

Wozniak, Steve and Gina Smith, *iWoz. Computer Geek to Cult Icon: How I Invented the Personal Computer, Co-Founded Apple, and Had Fun Doing It* (New York, 2006)

Yates, JoAnne, 'The Structuring of Early Computer Use in Life Insurance', *Journal of Design History*, XII/1 (1999), pp. 5–24

Acknowledgements

Some of the ideas and arguments in this book have been developed over a number of years, and have been presented in papers given at conferences around the world as well as published in a different form in academic journals. I am grateful to the audiences of those conferences and in particular the editors, editorial boards and blind reviewers of the journals *Design Issues*, *History and Technology* and the *Journal of Design History* for their invaluable advice and feedback. For helpful editorial advice in the writing of this book, my thanks go to Vivian Constantinopoulos and Martha Jay at Reaktion Books.

Part of the research for this book was funded by a grant from the British Academy, for which I am very grateful. I am also indebted to the University of Huddersfield and Sheffield Hallam University for their support during the research for and the writing of this book.

Personal thanks go to all those I have interviewed in the course of this research, including Celeste Baranski, Dennis Boyle, Paul Bradley, Kate Brinks, Stuart Card, John Ellenby, Doug Engelbart, Jeff Hawkins, Sam Hurst, Alan Kay, Peter Muller, John Neale, Ralph Sklarew, Rickson Sun, Bill Verplank and Jim Yerchenco for giving their time so generously; and to Jon Agar, Martin Campbell-Kelly and Nic Maffei for advice and direction. Thanks also go to the large number of people who provided images and permissions to use them, and in particular to Bernie Cavanagh at bccm.co.uk for his expert work in optimising them for reproduction. Special thanks go to Bill Moggridge, for his continuing support throughout my research, his personal insights, providing images and his help in contacting so many people in the design and computing industries.

Finally, my thanks go to all my colleagues, relatives and friends who have put up with me throughout this project, and most of all to Sandra, without whose love, support and encouragement, this book might never have been completed.

Photo Acknowledgements

The author and publishers wish to express their thanks to the below sources of illustrative material and/or permission to reproduce it:

Bob Albrecht/DigiBarn Computer Museum: p. 157 (left); photos by Paul Atkinson: pp. 120 (original packaging), 128; Archivo Storico Olivetti, Ivrea, Italy: pp. 55, 220; British Cartooon Archive/Express Syndication: p. 196; British Cartoon Archive/Solo Syndication: p. 195; photograph by Keith Collie: p. 147; courtesy of Colossus Rebuild Limited: p. 31; courtesy of the Computer History Museum: pp. 14, 80, 90, 99, 101, 112, 113 right, 176 left, 223, 224; Design Council, courtesy of University of Brighton Design Archives (www.brighton.ac.uk/designarchives): p. 188; courtesy of Rick Dickinson: p. 165 (left); from the private collection of John Ellenby: pp. 176 right, 178; courtesy of Doug Engelbart Institute: pp. 64, 65; photos by Rick English: pp. 74, 122, 127; photo by Don Fogg: p. 105; courtesy of HP: pp. 76, 130, 169; courtesy of HP/Design Council: p. 17 (right); courtesy of IBM: pp. 11, 42, 43, 58, 69 (right), 102, 124, 214 foot; courtesy of IDEO: pp. 72, 104, 105, 117 right, 119, 123, 132; courtesy of IMSAI Division, Fischer-Freitas Company: p. 85; David C. Morrill/courtesy of IBM: p. 75; Erik Klein, vintage-computer.com: pp. 82, 83; photo KPA/Zuma/Rex Features: p. 231; photos courtesy of Markene Kruse-Smith, Atari Home Computers Editor/Writing Manager: pp. 163, 225; courtesy of Nokia: p. 131; courtesy of NPL, © Crown copyright 1950: p. 38; image courtesy of NS&I: p. 191; The Ogilvy Group: p. 227 top right; courtesy of OLPC: p. 109; Panasonic Toughbook (www.toughbook.edu): p. 181; photos used with permission of PARC (Palo Alto Research Center, Inc.): pp. 68 (left), 69 (left), 95; John Plimmer, Japics Ltd: p. 171 top; photo Rex Features: p. 134; Bryan Roppolo (ti994.com): p. 227 foot; by courtesy of the Science Fiction Foundation Collection, University of Liverpool Library (ref no. PX1000.A873): pp. 200, 218; Science Museum, London/Science & Society Picture Library: pp. 25, 70, 86; photo Sipa Press/Rex Features: p. 168; Len Shustek & Jim Mehl/DigiBarn Computer Museum: p. 157 (right); courtesy of Dr Ralph Sklarew/Peter H. Muller, Inter4m: p. 117 left; courtesy of Sony: p. 179; photo by Steven Stengel/adapted by Bernie Cavanagh: p. 88; photo by Steven Stengel/oldcomputers.net: p. 89; courtesy of Ivan Sutherland: p. 113 left; Alastair Sweeny/blackberryplanetbook.com: p. 133; Used by Permission of Tyco

Index